A CONTRIBUTION TO THE DEBATE ON THE MEANING OF THE PLACE-NAME KM.T

AFRICAN SCHOLASTIC HOMELAND SECURITY AGENCY

A Contribution to the Debate on the Meaning of the Place-Name Km.t

The Shemsu Heru Research Team

Madu-Ndela Press
Philadelphia

2019

ABOUT THE AUTHORS

Sonjedi Ankh Ra (Ifátundé 'Fáyemí) is a medical technician and an independent researcher in Africana Studies with a concentration in ancient Kemet. His initial Kemetic studies took place under Ankh Mi Ra, author of *Let the Ancestors Speak: Removing the Veil of Mysticism from the Medew Netcher*. He continued his education with the Kera ("shrine") Jhuty Heru Neb Hu under Mfundishi: Jhutyms Ka n Heru Hassan Kamau Salim, which included Medu Netcher and Kiswahili language studies. Sonjedi's experience also includes studies with Sebat: Rkhty Amen, as well as Òrìṣà studies under Olúwo: Obáfemi 'Fáyemí Epega. He is currently the royal scribe for the Temple of Anu and the Serudj Tawi, a coalition of Kemetic spiritual houses.

Wudjau Men-Ib Iry-Maat is a computer programmer and graphic designer from Washington D.C. whose research focus is the engagement of the Ancient Egyptian civilization and culture through its languages. He is the founder of the Scribal Institute: Seshew Maa Ny Medew Netcher and a noted teacher of the Ancient Egyptian language and Hieroglyphic writing system. He is the author of the text book A *Beginner's Introduction To Medew Netcher - The Ancient Egyptian Hieroglyphic System, Ancient Egyptian Orthography & Grammar - A Synchronic Descriptive Grammar of the Older Speech of Kemet,* and *Has The Egyptian Hieroglyphic Writing System Been De- ciphered? – A Rebuttal To Walter Williams*.

Asar Imhotep is a software developer, Cultural Theorist and Africana researcher from Houston, TX whose research focus is the cultural, linguistic and philosophical links between the Ancient Egyptian civilizations and modern Bantu cultures of central and South Africa. He has a B.A. in Computer Information Systems (CIS) from the University of Houston, with a double minor in African-American and African studies. He is currently continuing his education in Computer Science with a concentration in Artificial Intelligence. He is the author of such works as *Where is the Love? How language can reorient us back to love's purpose* (2015), and *Nsw.t Bjt.j (King) in Ancient Egyptian: A lesson in paronymy and leadership* (2016). He has contributed chapters to academic works including *The Encyclopedia of African Religion* (2008) edited by Molefi Asante and Ama Mazama; and *Unite et Pluralite de la Verite: Melanges en l'Honneur du Prof. Dr. Alphonse Ngindu Mushete, Vol. I* (2014) edited by R. Malaba Mpoyi and Kalamba Nsapo. Asar Imhotep is a frequent contributor and presenter at the Cheikh Anta Diop International Conferences, and was also presented the DISA Award for "Intellectual Initiative and Academic Action" in 2015.

A Madu-Ndela Press Book
www.asarimhotep.com

Interior and Composition: Harold Johnson
MOCHA Design Studios

ISBN-13: 978-1094749921

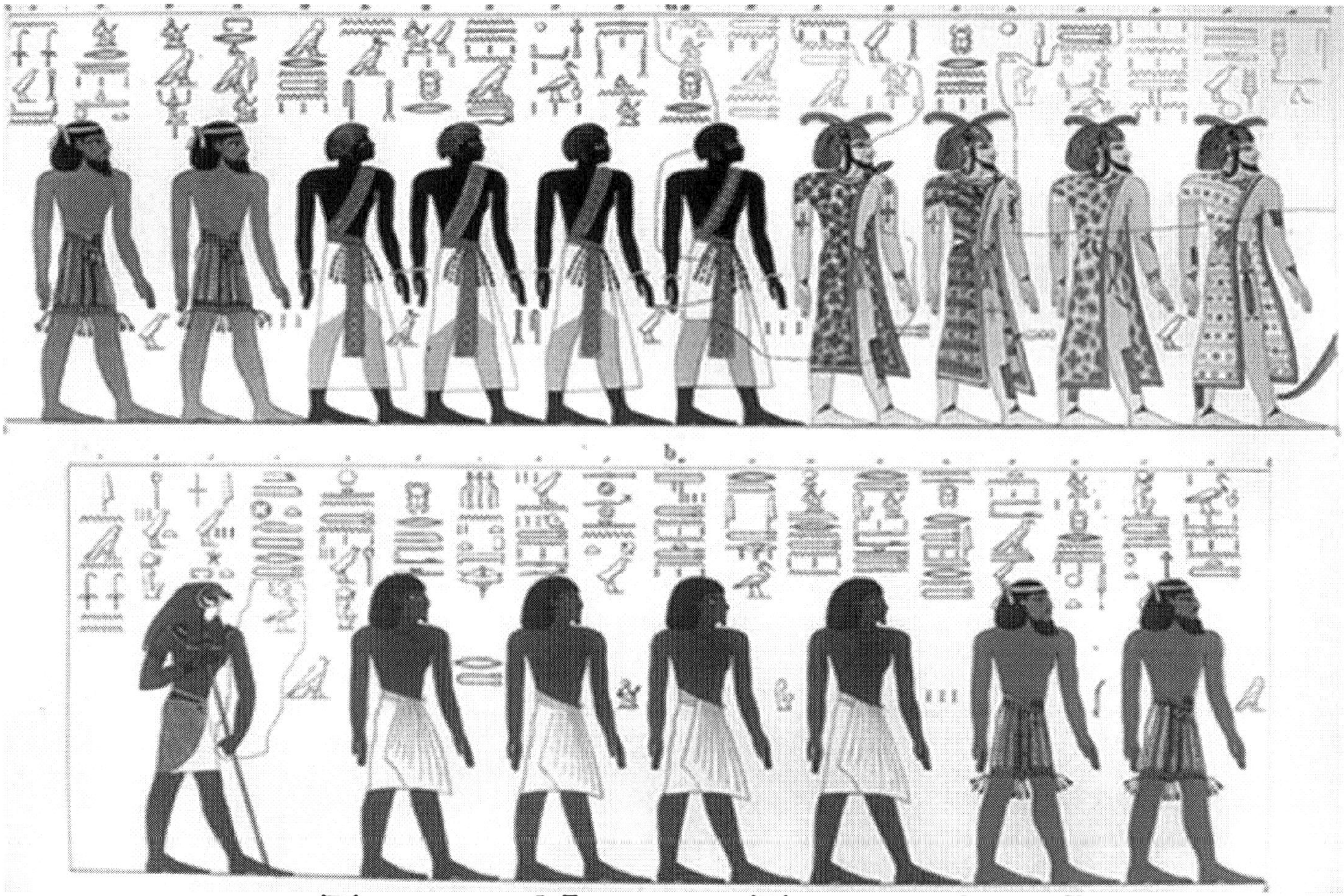

- Table of Nations, Tomb of Seti I -

TABLE OF CONTENTS

Introduction

The present volume is a collection of essays that seek to provide some answers to a long-standing debate in Egyptology concerning the meaning, history, and application of one of the many names of ancient Egypt: i.e., *km.t* 𓆎𓅓𓏏𓊖. Two working hypotheses have dominated the Egyptological literature. Hypothesis 1 argues that *km.t* means "the black land," referring to the color of the alluvial deposits left after the flood waters of the Nile River has receded. This hypothesis has been with us since the beginning of the discipline of Egyptology. Hypothesis 2 argues that *km.t* means "black people" and refers to the skin color of the ancient Egyptians. This hypothesis originates with the late Cheikh Anta Diop who argued this point at the famous Cairo Symposium held in 1974 in Cairo Egypt. Both hypotheses assume that the word *km.t* derives from a root *km* (adj.) 𓆎𓅓 "black."

As a result of the hypothesis provided by Diop (1977), heated debates have arisen—both in and outside academia—concerning the merits of both proposals. It was in the heat of the great controversy surrounding Martin Bernal's text *Black Athena: The Afroasiatic Roots of Classical Civilization, Vol. I* (1987) in the 1990's that brought the meaning of the place-name *km.t* to the public for debate. *Black Athena* caused a stir among Classicists because it argued, in part, that Greek civilization owed much of its intellectual and cultural heritage to Semitic speaking cultures in southwest Asia and the ancient Egyptians in north Africa. But more controversial, at least for some Eurocentric academics, was Bernal's (somewhat) support for the notion that the ancient Egyptians were "black" in phenotype (Bernal, 1987: 242). It is the latter point that caused the most issues among European academics, primarily because it appears to support the arguments by Afrocentric scholars (e.g., James 1954, Diop 1974, 1991; Obenga 1992, Ben-Jochannan 1972, Asante 1990, Williams 1992) who claimed that: 1) the ancient Egyptians were Black African people, and 2) that Egypt played a significant role in the development of ancient Greek philosophy. The fight for *Black Athena* was essentially the fight for the origin of Western civilization as we know it.

Scholars from around the world chimed in on the debate: each arguing for or against specific points brought out in *Black Athena* (1987). There was even a United Kingdom television documentary in 1991 simply titled "Black Athena" that highlighted the issues of the debate up to that time. In 1996, Dr. Mary Lefkowitz (Professor Emerita of Classical Studies at Wellesley College) wrote a text *Not Out of Africa: How "Afrocentrism" Became an Excuse to Teach Myth as History*[1] in response to both Bernel's *Black Athena* and the growing popularity of Afrocentric scholarship. Essentially, Lefkowitz accuses Afrocentric scholars of 'revisionist' history because they 1) dared to write about their own history, and 2) challenged the orthodox narrative of how modern civilization came to be. The debate was so heated that HarperCollins, the publisher of NOA, invited both Lefkowitz and Bernal to engage in an online academic debate on the issue. A special listserv was set up for the exchange. Central to the debate were two questions: were the ancient Egyptians a Black African people, and to what extent was the civilization of ancient Greece indebted (whether learned or 'stolen') to ancient Egypt? While both Lefkowitz and Bernal participated, their contribution was actually small. The bulk of the debate was actually carried out by a number of scholars from around the world. Below is a 1996 email advertising the event.

---

1 For now on written as NOA.

"The Athena Debate"

THE ATHENA DEBATE: HISTORY CAUGHT IN THE CLASSICAL CROSSFIRE

For the first time in an electronic forum, Mary Lefkowitz, author of *Not Out of Africa: How Afrocentrism Became an Excuse to Teach Myth as History* and Martin Bernal, author of *Black Athena*, will debate, with participating scholars, modern ideas of the origins of Western Civilization, the fate of academic standards and the threat to academic freedom.

This debate will run from April 22nd through the month of May and will be sponsored by Basic Books, an imprint of HarperCollins Publishers. We invite you to subscribe to this free debate by sending an e-mail message to:

lists@info.harpercollins.com
In the body of the message, write:

subscribe athena
(Be sure that no other words or characters appear in the message you send.)
For more information, contact:
gay.salisbury@harpercollins.com
- -
Date: Tue, 2 Apr 1996 16:49:04 GMT-5 From: H-AFRICA---Mel Page <AFRICA@ETSUARTS.EAST-TENN-ST.EDU> Subject: NET: "The Athena Debate"[2]

After this listserv was shut down by HarperCollins, other listservs and Yahoogroups emerged to keep the conversation going. In both the HarperCollins listserv and the subsequent listservs that followed, Afrocentric scholars were relying on the arguments of Diop (1977) to counter the Eurocentric onslaught against the discipline of Africology. We recall that one of the core questions for the debate was, "Were the ancient Egyptians a Black African people?" In defense of the affirmative to this question, Afrocentric scholars relied heavily on Diop (1977, 1991), which argued that not only were the Egyptians 'black'—as evidenced by the depictions of themselves on the walls of Egypt, and by the testimony of the Greeks on the phenotype of the Egyptians—but also because (as Diop claimed) the Egyptians called themselves Black as evidenced by the name of the country: i.e., Km.t 𓆎𓅓𓏏𓊖. However, as stated previously, Diop did not argue from the standpoint of orthodox Egyptology that the word Km.t meant "black land." Instead he argued that Km.t meant "black people." Another argument that many of the Afrocentric scholars were using against the Eurocentric researchers is that Km.t could not mean "black land" because it was never determined by classifiers for "land." Instead, they read the O49 𓊖 glyph in Km.t 𓆎𓅓𓏏𓊖 as a "city plan" depiction and related it to "people" as *occupants* of a city. Thus, as a result of the *Black Athena* debates, Diop's position travelled around the world and became a staple part of the larger debate on the racial makeup of the ancient Egyptians.

It is in the year 1998 that Asar Imhotep (one of the main contributors to this volume) graduated high school and entered Southwest Texas State University (now Texas State University). It was there where he was introduced to all of the above information via a reading of the then still lively online debates. After a number of years of passively observing and reading through the arguments, at around the year 2000-2001 Asar Imhotep began to engage the discourse with his own inquiries and arguments. It was in 2002 that he presented his first paper at an academic conference[3] on the subject titled "What's in a name? The meaning of Km.t." In this text Imhotep rejected the idea that Km.t meant either "the black land" or "black people." Instead he argued that more than likely the place-name had a relationship to the *šms.w-ḥr.w* 𓌞𓅱𓁷𓏥𓅃 or "followers of Heru" [Wb 4, 486.16-19; LGG VII, 91 f.; vgl. LÄ III, 51 f.] who were blacksmiths who came from the south. At the time Imhotep was still in agreeance with the argument that Km.t derived from a root *km* 𓆎𓅓𓁐 "black." Instead of the blackness being related to the soil or color of the people, he argued, it more than likely was in reference to an occupation of blacksmithing. This was based on the argument by Diop (1977, 1991) that the I6 *km* 𓆎

2 A copy of this facsimile is currently held on the University of Pennsylvania, African Studies Center website: http://www.africa.upenn.edu/Listserv/athenalist.html.

3 The African-American Studies Symposium at the University of Houston in Houston, TX.

grapheme represented a single piece of burning coal [Wb 5, 122.10].

As time progressed, and new academic skillsets were obtained,[4] Imhotep began to abandon his original hypotheses that he argued in 2002. He still argued that Km.t did not mean "black land" or "black people." However, his most recent arguments maintain that Km.t had nothing to do with blackness at all, but with *fertile land* due to the presence of an abundance of water and vegetation from a river or heavy rains (see Imhotep 2008, 2010, 2014, 2016). Imhotep rejected the two major hypotheses concerning the meaning of the place-name Km.t primarily due to poor methodology and faulty logic. In short, he was just not convinced of the prevailing arguments. Since Imhotep (2002), a number of African scholars have independently analyzed the meaning of the place-name Km.t and have rejected both hypotheses 1 and 2, instead relating Km.t to a type of land or country with no color connotation: e.g., Pfouma (2007), Sambu (2007, 2011), Mboli (2010), and Bilolo (p.c.: 2010). We briefly examine each hypothesis below.

When we critically examine the nature of both hypotheses, we discover that both arguments display a clear case of the *Begging the Question* logical fallacy.

Hypothesis 1:

James P. Allen, *Middle Egyptian: An Introduction to the Language and Culture of Hieroglyphs* (2010: 345)[5] states the following:

> The word *kmt* "Egypt," literally means "black," referring to the soil of the Nile Valley (see Essay 2). This is why Egyptian uses the preposition *ḥr* "on" rather than *m* "in": *ḥr kmt* means literally "on the black land."

The primary source Allen is referring to comes from the *Tale of Sinuhe* (R. 50):

sjꜣ *.n* *wj* *mjtn* *jm* *pꜣ* *wnn* *ḥr kmt*

"The scout there, who had once been in Egypt, recognized me."

Here Allen simply repeats the orthodox explanation for the term Km.t, but doesn't provide any proof that it is the case. He assumes that Km.t derives from *km* "black" simply based on paronymy: i.e., similarity of forms of two words that may or may not derive from a common root.

Hypothesis 2:

Cheikh Anta Diop, in his translated article "Origin of the Ancient Egyptians," states the following:

> The Egyptians had only one term to designate themselves: *km.t* = the negros (literally). In the Egyptian language, a word of assembly is formed from an adjective or a noun by putting it in the feminine singular. 'Kmt' from the adjective *km* = black; it therefore means strictly negroes or at the very least black men. The term is a collective noun which thus described the whole people of Pharaonic Egypt as a black people. (Ivan Van Sertima, 1986: 46-48)

In the case of Diop (1986), we can break down his argument into the following logical sequences:

- **Premise 1**: The Egyptians had only one term to designate themselves: *km.t* = the negros (literally).
- **Premise 2**: a word of assembly is formed from an adjective or a noun by putting it in the feminine singular.
- **Premise 3**: 'Kmt' from the adjective *km* = black;
- **Conclusion**: it [Km.t] therefore means strictly negroes or at the very least black men.

---

4 For example, the ability to read the *sš-md.w-nṯr* (hieroglyphs), a strong background in historical comparative linguistics, and proper scientific research methodology provided his background in computer science.

5 This is just one example out of hundreds as the example provided by Allen (2010) is representative of the standard response in Egyptology.

What we witness here is what is called a *begging the question* logical fallacy. This argument is fallacious, in part, because it does not offer an independent reason for the claim he is trying to support (the 'dependency' problem). In other words, Diop (and essentially all Egyptologists) is trying to support something by supposing proved what he has yet to be proved. When determining whether we have a case of this logical fallacy, we must ask ourselves the following questions:

1. Has the arguer avoided the obligation to provide independent support for a claim by restating it in similar terms?
2. Has an arguer avoided the obligation to provide independent support by assuming somewhere in the premises the very thing that has to be shown?

We must ask of each premise *the grounds* on which we are asked to accept it as true and valid. Asking this question will expose cases in which we discover that the grounds by which we should accept a premise is the very point that we are supposed to see being proved in the conclusion (Tindale, 2007: 75-76). Where we can show this to occur, we have detected an instance of the fallacy of *Begging the Question*.

What Imhotep discovered as a result of critically examining all of the previous arguments is that no scholar had attempted to prove that Km.t meant "black land" or "black people" using sound and established methods in the field of etymology. Given the magnitude of the debate, one would have expected that everyone involved would have gone through a scientific process to answer definitively the underlying question. What was simply the case is that the early pioneers of Egyptology formulated hypotheses concerning the meaning and application of the place-name Km.t, but they did not go about confirming their hypotheses. Instead, the Egyptological community (on both ends) uncritically accepted these hypotheses without conducting any independent research to corroborate the claims made by the early Egyptologists. As a result, the vast majority of the Egyptological literature today simply accepts as fact these unproven hypotheses and it is this uncritical acceptance that has contributed to the ongoing debate concerning the name Km.t. The debate is ongoing, and the arguments circular, because the rigorous scientific method has not been applied to this research question: "What is the meaning of the place-name Km.t?" Imhotep took it upon himself to apply the rigors of the scientific method in an effort to come to a more definitive answer to this question. His latest results will be published in the Fall of 2019 in the text *Aaluja, Vol. II: Cyena-Ntu Religion and Philosophy* (Madu-Ndela Press).

It is this background that has brought us here today. After engaging in a number of public and private debates on the subject, Imhotep and colleagues Wudjau Iry-Ma'at (Atlanta, GA) and Sonjedi Ankh Ra (Philadelphia, PA), have agreed to make arguments against hypotheses 1 and 2 at the *36th Annual Ancient Kemetic (Egyptian) Studies Conference* organized by ASCAC[6] at Medgar Evans College in Brooklyn, NY April 18-21. Defending the position of Diop's Hypothesis 2 will be Dr. Mario Beatty (Washington, DC), Bro. Reggie Mabrey (New York, NY), and Neter-Neb (Baltimore, MD). Given that each researcher has only 20 minutes to present their case, and that the nature of the question is very complex—which would take hours to explain to a lay audience the intimate details of the matter—Imhotep, Iry-Ma'at, and Ankh-Ra decided to create and make available this publication as an extension of their 2019 ASCAC presentations. These chapters will help fill in the gaps that are anticipated due to time constraints at the conference.

The principle purpose of this text is to demonstrate how the focused, multidisciplinary research of the authors, working continuously in this area for a period of approximately 20 years, has been able to contribute to the field of Egyptology. This text, *A Contribution to the Debate on the Meaning of the Place-Name Km.t* (2019) is not intended to be a complete argument regarding the etymology of Km.t. This will take place in Imhotep (2019) mentioned previously. For now, we define M-E ***km.t*** to mean "a riparian land; a pasturage with an abundance of grass and water," with cognates in Sumerian ***ki****.duru* "damp ground; irrigable land" and CiLuba ***ci****.nkanda* "piece of land; field; part of land being plowed in a day" (in other words, "farm land").

The central concern in this volume is in educating the lay public on the methodologies, understandings, and considerations needed to *answer* the research question on the meaning of Km.t. It is a prelude to the larger work to come. This volume, then, is pursued as a contribution to the development of sound research

6 The Association for the Study of Classical African Civilizations.

strategies needed to answer questions regarding lexical items of an obscure semantic nature that we do not fully understand. As this project is open-textured, it is also an invitation to others for intellectual engagement and challenge. Our hope is that our little contribution expands the discourse regarding ancient Egyptian culture, language, and psychology. While the authors do not claim to end the debate with this publication, we hope that it will, however, improve the quality of debate regarding the meaning of Km.t.

Selected Bibliography

ALLEN, James P. (2005). *The Ancient Egyptian Pyramid Texts*. Society of Biblical Literature. Atlanta, GA.

______ (2010). *Middle Egyptian: An Introduction into the Language and Culture of Hieroglyphs*, 2nd Edition. Cambridge University Press. Cambridge.

ASANTE, Molefi. (1990). *Kemet, Afrocentricity and Knowledge*. Africa World Press. Chicago., IL

BERNAL, Martin. (1987). *Black Athena: The Afroasiatic Roots of Classical Civilization, Vol. I – The Frabrication of Ancient Greece* (1785-1985). Rutgers University Press. NJ.

BEN-JOCHANNAN, Yosef. A.A. (1972). *Black Man of the Nile and His Family*. Black Classic Press. Baltimore, MD.

DIOP, Cheikh A. (1974). *The African Origin of Civilization: Myth or Reality*. Lawrence Hill & Co. NY.

______ (1977). *Parenté génétique de l'Egyptien pharaonique et des langues négro-africaines: processus de sémitisation*. Les Nouvelles Éditions Africaines. Ifan-Dakar.

______ (1991). *Civilization or Barbarism: An Authentic Anthropology*. Chicago Review Press. Chicago, IL.

GARDINER. Alan H. (2007). *Egyptian Grammar: Being an Introduction to the Study of Hieroglyphs*, 3rd edition. Friffith Institute Oxford. Cambridge.

IMHOTEP, Asar. (2012). "Egypt in its African Context Note 3: Towards a Method for Vocalizing *mdw nṯr* Symbols." Unpublished.

______ (2013). *Aaluja: Rescue, Reinterpretation and the Restoration of Major Ancient Egyptian Themes, Vol.* MOCHA-Versity Press. Houston, TX.

______ (2014). "A lesson in Egyptian Determinatives: The case of Km.t." Unpublished.

______ (2015). *Where is the Love? How language can reorient us back to love's purpose*. MOCHA-Versity Press. Houston, TX.

______ (2016). *Nsw.t Bjt.j (King) in Ancient Egyptian: A lesson in paronymy and leadership*. Madu-Ndela Press. Philadelphia, PA.

______ (2019). *Aaluja, Vol. II: Cyena-Ntu Religion and Philosophy*. Madu-Ndela Press. Philadelphia.

LEFKOWITZ, Mary. (1996). *Not Out of Africa: How Afrocentrism Became an Excuse to Teach Myth as History*. Basic Books.

LOPRIENO, Antonio. (1995). *Ancient Egyptian: A Linguistic Introduction.* Cambridge University Press. New York, NY.

MBOLI, Jean-Claude. (2010). *Origine des langues africaines: Essai d'application de la méthode comparative aux langues africaines anciennes et modernes*. L'Harmattan. Paris.

OBENGA, Theophile. (1992). *Ancient Egypt & Black Africa: A Student's Handbook for the Study of Ancient Egypt in Philosophy, Linguistics & Gender Relations*. Karnak House. London.

______ (1993). *Origine commune de l'égyptien ancien, du copte et des langues négro-africaines modernes – Introduction à la linguistique historique africaine*. L'Harmattan. Paris.

PFOUMA, Oscar, "Aegyptio-Graphica VI. L'abeille et le pays Apuntes de Egiptologia," (*AdE*) n°2, Asuncion, 2007, 45-48.

SAMBU, Kipkoeech A. (2008). *The Kalenjiin People's Egypt Origin Legend Revisited: Was Isis Asiis?* 2nd Edition. Longhorn Publishers. Nairobi, Kenya.

______ (2011). *The Misiri Legend Explored: A Linguistic Inquiry into the Kalenjiin People's Oral Tradition of Ancient Egypt*. University of Nairobi Press. Nairobi, Kenya.

TINDALE, Christopher W. (2007). *Fallacies and Argument Appraisal*. Cambridge University Press. Cambridge.

VAN-SERTIMA, Ivan. (Ed.). (1986). Great African Thinkers: Cheikh Anta Diop. The Journal of African Civilizations. New Jersey.

WILLIAMS, Chancellor. (1974). *The Destruction of Black Civilization: Great Issues of a Race from 4500 B.C. to 2000 A.D.* Third World Press. Chicago, IL.

Chapter I: Methodological considerations in establishing the meaning of Km.t

Asar Imhotep

> I would like to see above all a greater number of researchers—Afroamericans—young Americans—and even whites. Why not? Because it's the young who are the least prejudiced. As a consequence, they are the most capable of making triumph ideas which frighten the older generation. Also, I think that it will be necessary to put together polyvalent scientific teams, capable of doing in-depth studies, for sure, and that's what's important. It bothers me when someone takes me on my word without developing a means of verifying what I say . . . We must form a scientific spirit capable of seeing even the weaknesses of our own proofs, of seeing the unfinished side of our work and of committing ourselves to completing it. You understand? Therefore we should then have a work which could honestly stand criticism, because what we've done would have been placed on a scientific plane.
>
> —Cheikh Anta Diop[1]

Introduction

The principle purpose of this chapter is to discuss and delineate the *methodology* needed to answer the question, "What is the etymology and meaning of the place-name *km.t* in the ancient Egyptian language?" As discussed in the Introduction, the debate on the meaning of *km.t* has been prolonged due to a lack of a systematic analysis of the hypotheses presented by various scholars over the years. Many arguments have been presented accompanied by unproven assumptions. It is these assumptions that have altered the trajectory of the researcher, veering him off course from the path of the truth. This chapter is aimed at the young researcher who may be interested in answering similar research questions in the near future and are looking for tools of analysis to help them solve their etymological problems.

Statement of the Problem

The place-name Km.t is a toponym of obscure meaning. Due to its similarity in form to a word *km(m)* "black," researchers have assumed that the latter is the root of the former. However, there are other words in the Egyptian language with the *k-m* consonant sequence (homographs) that are just as likely candidates to be the root of Km.t. These possibilities have not been explored historically. While there are a few researchers who have analyzed the use of the toponym in ancient Egyptian texts (e.g., Goelet 1999, Nibbi 1997), there has not been a systematic *linguistic* analysis of the term and its possible origin using the historical comparative method. The work of Imhotep (2019) aims to solve this problem. This chapter, however, concerns itself with *some* of the *considerations* that went into the complete analysis on the subject discussed in Imhotep (2019).

The importance of methodology

Methodology, according to McDougal (2014: 30), is the aspect of research that contains the paradigms, theories, concepts, and methods[2] that shape approaches to study and social intervention. It is the methodology

1 Harun Kofi Wangura, "Interview with Cheikh Anta Diop," In: *Black World*, Vol. XXIII, No. 4. February, 1974, pp. 57-58. This answer was in response to the question of, "What sort of preparations should young scholars make to undertake future studies in the field of Africology/African-Studies?"

2 Methods are the tools of data collection.

that the researcher is guided by that determines what assumptions is made, the choice of research method, what questions are asked, what questions are not asked, and what theories are used to make sense of the data collected. Two major components of research methodology are *paradigms* and *theories*. Paradigms, in essence, is the conceptual universe or framework that guides descriptions, explanations and evaluations of the empirical world. A paradigm, thus, is a general way of understanding and approaching knowledge of the world (McDougal, 2014: 32). Theories, on the other hand, are interrelated sets of propositions whose aim is to explain some aspect of reality. Theories are inspired by observations and people seek to carry out scientific experiments to verify their observations. It is through this process that one discovers *facts* (things that are known or proved to be true). Theories, therefore, seeks to explain the interrelationship between some facts, as well as a given set of *concepts* (abstract ideas that enable one to categorize data).

Scientific research consists of people making systemic observations and testing those observations to ultimately develop or strengthen a theory. A theory gains strength and validity the more it has been tested and verified. Researchers look for patterns and trends in the data. A quality theory helps to better explain the observed patterns and regularities, as well as why those regularities occur. Any scientific explanation has to be *testable*: that is, there must be possible observational consequences that could support the theory, hypothesis, etc. But most importantly, it must also be *falsifiable*: that is, it must be framed in a way that some observational evidence could potentially count against it. It is the latter point that underscores the importance of proper research methodology.

When a researcher releases a paper on a particular subject, he or she understands that from that point on, other scholars will make it their business to scrutinize and tear apart their central arguments. This isn't done out of malice or hatred. It is part of the scientific process. It is the natural tension needed to help researchers refine and tune arguments and experiments that help us to get closer to the truth. In science, observations and explanations build on each other. It, therefore, is a cumulative activity. The objective of sound research design is to develop and incorporate procedures and paradigms that help our argument survive the critical review process from other scholars. Scientists only have one objective, one important goal and that is to *know the truth*. Arguments that can survive scrutiny bring us all closer to knowing the truth, which is why the attempted falsification by fellow researchers is an important and necessary component of the scientific process.

Because of the intense verification process in the many different scientific fields, academic research has been likened to warfare; primarily because one is constantly in a battle with other arguments vying to hold the position of THE theory that best explains some aspect of reality. It is a type of "intellectual warfare," to use the language of Jacob Carruthers. While real warfare and scientific research are vastly different entities, they do share some similarities: a few I'd like to exploit here.

When two armies are engaged in warfare, it is common knowledge that the enemy is going to try every which way to disrupt or eliminate three essential assets needed for an army to survive and win the war: i.e., communications, food/water, and supplies.[3] Without these essentials, no army can have hopes of winning the war. The truth of this fact can be seen in a speech that the former President of the United States George W Bush (Jr.) conducted on October 7, 2001 attempting to justify his decision to attack Afghanistan after the September 11th attacks that killed thousands of U.S. citizens. In his speech he says the following:

> §5 More than two weeks ago, I gave Taliban leaders a series of clear and specific demands: Close terrorist training camps; hand over leaders of the al Qaeda network; and return all foreign nationals, including American citizens, unjustly detained in your country. None of these demands were met. And now the Taliban will pay a price.
>
> §6 **By destroying camps and disrupting communication, we will make it more difficult for the terror network to train new recruits and coordinate their evil plans.** Initially, the terrorists may burrow deeper into caves and other entrenched hiding places. Our military action is also designed to clear the way for sustained, comprehensive and relentless operations to drive them out and bring them to justice.

---

3 Some probably would add "morale" to this equation.

> §7 At the same time, the oppressed people of Afghanistan will know the generosity of America and our allies. As we strike military targets, we will also drop food, medicine and supplies to the starving and suffering men and women and children of Afghanistan.[4]

By successfully destroying training camps, the U.S. army would be able to prevent the Taliban troops from regrouping and coordinating future attacks. Normally weapons are also stored in such camps, thus cutting off weapons supplies. By cutting off communications systems, it prevents the Taliban army from communicating effectively. These measures help to keep the other army confused and weakens their ability to strategize effectively when inevitable changes occur during the war.

In many respects, intellectual warfare follows the same pattern. However, instead of cutting off water and supplies, 'hostile' researchers will seek to attack one's methodology and bibliographic resources. These are the first things a researcher will attack. Therefore, to survive the onslaught of criticism to your argument, one's methodology must be strong and carefully crafted. It is an essential component needed to win the 'war' (i.e., a sound and lasting thesis). If one's methodology is not sound or erroneous, then one's conclusion will therefore be false. We have a saying in computer science, "Trash in, trash out" and this applies to research in general. One cannot expect to get a quality output if their inputs are subpar. In the case of the etymology of the place-name *km.t*, the ongoing debate has suffered from a lack of proper methodology and not knowing what tools to use to come to a sound conclusion. Most literature on the subject are in reality people's opinions. But none of these opinions were carried out using the scientific method, which would have helped us solve this problem a very long time ago.

The scientific method

Science is the use of evidence to construct testable explanations and predictions of natural phenomena, as well as the knowledge generated through this process.[5] In short, science is a way of *knowing* that depends on empirical evidence and testable explanations. Central to the scientific process is the use of *hypothesis testing*. A hypothesis is a suggested explanation for an event, which can be tested. They are tentative explanations and generally are produced within the context of a scientific theory. A *scientific theory* is a generally accepted, thoroughly tested and confirmed explanation for a set of observations or phenomena. Repeatable observations and experiments generate explanations that describe nature more accurately and comprehensively. These observations, in turn, suggest new observations and experiments that can be used to test and extend the explanation. Within this context, scientific explanations improve over time. Subsequent generations of scientists work to correct, refine, and extend the work done by their predecessors.

There cannot be science without a proper, rigorous, and systematic methodology for determining reality. This systematic procedure for theory development is known as *the scientific method,* which has characterized natural science since the 17th century. The scientific method is a method of procedure and a set of principles consisting in systematic observation, measurement, and experiment, and the formulation, testing, and modification of hypotheses. There is no one standard process for the scientific method and it really just depends on what discipline one is researching in that will determine what procedures one will use and in what order. But typically, the scientific method consists of the following steps:

4 A full facsimile of the speech can be found here: https://www.press.uchicago.edu/Misc/Chicago/481921texts.html. (Retrieved 4/11/2019).

5 National Academy of Sciences Institute of Medicine, *Science, Evolution, and Creationism*, (Washington, DC: The National Academies Press), 2008, p. 10.

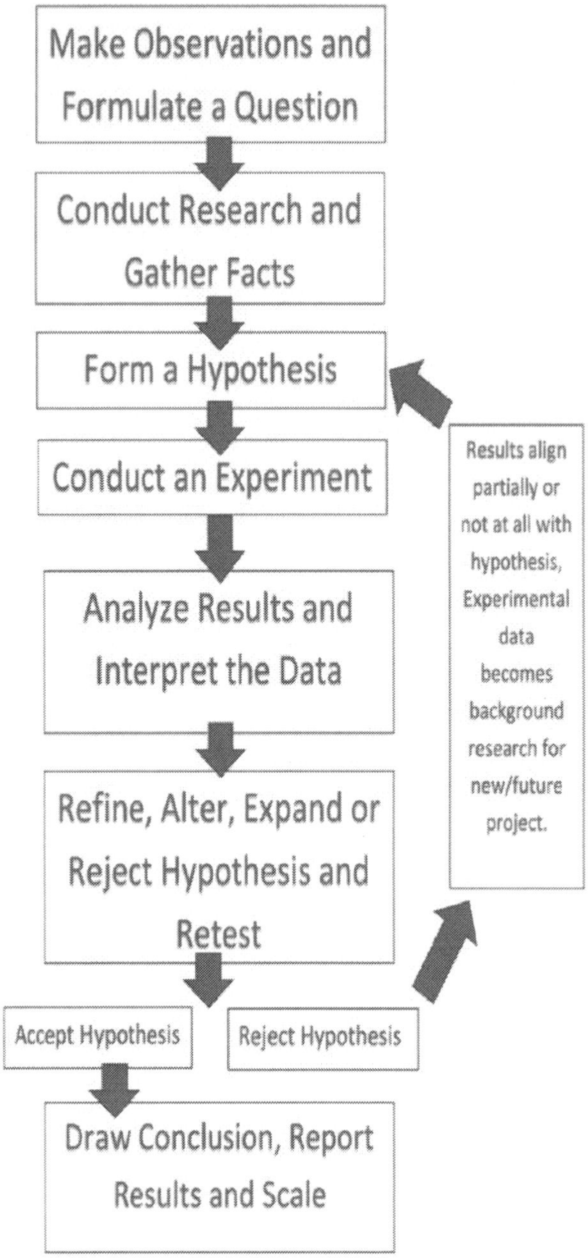

Fig. 1: Steps in the scientific method

Science values results that are verifiable and reproducible as the basis for knowledge. It is because of this essential value that scientists, in their research results, inform us of their methodology so that other scientists can reduplicate the observation or experiment to verify the initial results. By understanding the paradigms that shape an experiment, one can understand what guides a researcher's development of theories and their conduct of research.

One of the major purposes for the scientific method is the generation and falsification of hypotheses. Scientists do not seek to confirm hypotheses, but to *refute* them through observation and experimentation. The better a hypothesis is able to withstand falsification (under highly controlled conditions), the more likely it will be accepted as an accurate reflection of reality and can be used in the development, or strengthening, of a (given) theory. Hypotheses must be quantifiable, testable, and have predictive value. One purpose of the scientific method is to eliminate chance as an explanation for the results we observe. Another purpose is to eliminate, as much as humanly possible, human bias that may taint the results of an experiment.

The Importance of the Comparative Method

Determining the proper research design depends on the nature of the research question being asked. In our case, our research question is: "What is the etymology and meaning of the place-name *km.t*?" The nature of the question will tell us under what scientific field of inquiry our research will be conducted, and ultimately what tools of analysis will be necessary to answer the question. Given that we are seeking the *etymology* and *meaning* of a place-name (i.e., a toponym), we know that our question is a *linguistic* one and only the tools of linguistics will allow us to answer the question. Provided that this is a linguistic question, one would be hard-pressed to find the solution to the linguistic problem by turning on the Large Hadron Collider at CERN in Switzerland. Like with any repair project, you are going to need the right tools for the job. For our inquiry, our primary tools of analysis are *the historical comparative method* and *semantics*. Other tools can be used to help solve the problem (e.g., art theory). But the primary onus are the tools of linguistics.

When it comes to trying to solve the riddle of the meaning of *km.t*, scholars have been reluctant to utilize the tools of linguistics to answer this question. The great linguist and theologian Modupe Oduyoye, in his *Words and Meaning in Yorùbá Religion* (1996), warned us about neglecting linguistics in our attempts at understanding ancient cultures. He states that:

> [A]ny student of African beliefs or of any preliterate society who does not have this tool [philology/ linguistics] is severely handicapped; **any researcher who undervalues it does so at his own peril.** For "language has preserved for us the inner, living history of man's soul." Emphasize "living." "Language has been described as the oldest living witness to history." Without linguistic corroboration, archaeological evidence is tantalizingly inarticulate. "And here is a challenge," to use Professor Ìdòwú's words, "each one of us must get to know his own people thoroughly and approach their belief reverently and sympathetically because we possess that which is the key to their soul—the language." (Oduyoye, 1996: 22) (bolded emphasis mine)

In other words, this tool of linguistics is critical to understanding a people's culture and worldview. But since we are concerned with etymology, we must utilize the process of historical comparative linguistics to trace the origin of the word and its evolution. That etymology is a branch of historical comparative linguistics is echoed by Philip Durkin in his *The Oxford Guide to Etymology* (2009).[6] When contextualizing who the text is written for, Durkin attempts:

> to frame this book so that it is addressed most centrally to someone who has an interest in ***historical linguistics*** . . . Etymology is a part of this wider field, and anyone's understanding of etymology will be greatly enriched by at least some acquaintance with the broader concerns of the discipline as a whole' (p. ix). (bolded emphasis mine)

This is important to note because there are several key areas for determining the etymology of a word in a given language that researchers have neglected to address when discussing the meaning of *km.t*. Thomas Krisch, in his essay "Etymology,"[7] discusses the origin of the process of etymology with the Greek philosopher Socrates and how it has evolved to the present day. In distinguishing how ancient and modern etymology is conducted, Krisch informs us that:

> The big difference between Socrates' approach and a 'modern' etymology is that nowadays one tries to argue systematically in all strata, in phonology, in morphology and in semantics/pragmatics and also

6 Philip Durkin, *The Oxford Guide to Etymology*, (Oxford: Oxford University Press), 2009, pp. x +350

7 In: Silvia Luraghi and Vit Bubenik (Eds.), *The Continuum Companion to Historical Linguistics*, (London, New York: Continuum International Publishing Group), pp. 311-322.

> extra-linguistically in philology and culture. One also takes into account historical developments. If one wants to be a productive and successful expert in etymology, one has to thoroughly study all the areas mentioned. (Luraghi & Bubenik, 2010: 313-314)

In other words, there are six areas of inquiry explored in the modern era when trying to find the etymology of a word in a given language. These six areas are *phonology* (the study of sound), *morphology* (the study of the structure of words), *semantics/pragmatics* (the study of meaning and context), *philology* (the study of texts), *history*, and *culture*. If one's analysis does not include the tools, theories, paradigms, and procedures from all six of these areas, then one is not doing (good) etymology.

Krisch goes on further to link etymology with historical comparative linguistics, like Durkin (2009) mentioned above. In underscoring the relationship between the two, Krisch informs us that:

> In the nineteenth and twentieth centuries (starting with Jacob Grimm, Franz Bopp and Rasmus Rask) the comparative method based on strict morphological, phonological and lexical comparison was developed. The most important output of this research was the discovery of sound laws which mediate between cognate languages, their respective older stages and their common predecessors. This research in turn relies on 'good' etymologies of words that exemplify the sound laws and the regularities of word formation. (Luraghi & Bubenik, 2010: 315)

Krisch introduces us to an important criterion when doing etymology: that is, the establishment of "sound laws" as a result of discovering regularities between form and meaning, in basic vocabulary, between two sets of languages. Part of why most Egyptologists are unable to solve the problem of Km.t is because they are not trained in historical comparative linguistics. When trying to answer the question on the meaning of *km.t*, most tried to answer it simply using the Egyptian language alone; without the establishment of any 'sound laws' from the comparison of Egyptian—which I call ciKam—and other related languages. Oduyoye warns us about this common practice and how it almost always leads to false conclusions.

> Another example of the limitation which a structuralist commitment imposed on Professor Bamgbose's attempt was a preliminary decision never to adduce words from any other language besides Yorùbá. Dialect forms were cited; but to cite words from other languages was considered to be wandering away from the field of Yorùbá studies. Structural linguistics inveighed against the practice of explaining one language in terms of another; structuralists believe that the full explanation of a language lies within that language. **This is an illusion**. And it is this illusion which separates the methods of Saussurian linguistics from the methods of classical philology. **Structuralism is monolingual, and a monolingual approach to etymology will always end up in folk etymology**. (Oduyoye, 1996: 43) (bolded emphasis mine)

Remember our axiom, "Trash in, trash out." This is essentially what Oduyoye (1996) is saying. By trying to answer an etymological question, which requires a comparative study with multiple languages, using a single language (trash in) always leads to folk-etymology (trash out). Folk-etymology is defined by Luraghi & Bubenik (2010: 375) as:

> The restructuring of a synchronically unanalyzable word or expression, so that its form allows for a semantic connection with other lexical items (e.g. if one reads 'life' into lifeguard which originally meant 'bodyguard'). Also called 'popular etymology.'

A Glossary of Historical Linguistics provides a more elaborate definition for folk-etymology as follows:

> **folk etymology** (also called popular etymology): A kind of analogical change in which speakers assign meaning associations to forms (words or morphemes) that the forms did not originally have based on their resemblance to other forms in the language, and on the basis of these new meaning associations either the original form is changed or new forms based on the new meaning associations are created.

> That is, speakers believe the word or morpheme to have an etymology or analysis that is false from the perspective of the form's earlier history. An example is the English word *hamburger*, whose true etymology is from German *Hamburg* + *-er*, 'someone from the city of Hamburg'; hamburgers are not made of 'ham', but speakers associated hamburger with ham and on this basis created new words such as cheeseburger, fishburger etc. Another example comes from the Spanish *vagabundo* 'vagabond, tramp', which gave rise in some varieties of Spanish to *vagamundo* 'tramp, vagabond', through the folk-etymological association with *vaga* 'wander, roam, loaf' and with *mundo* 'world'. See also *analogy*. (Campbell & Mixco, 2007: 65)

This is precisely what happened with the word *km.t* in the Egyptological literature. An example of folk-etymology in action can be seen among the Yorùbá; for when the recaptives from Freetown Sierra Leone, returned to Abeokuta and Lagos (Nigeria) with their new religion Christianity, the stay-at-home monolingual Yorùbá called those Creoles (Krio) *kiriyó* "Go about and get filled (with wine)" (Oduyoye, 1996: 11). Yorùbá folk thought the word *Creole* was analyzable (i.e., able to be broken down further) into the Yorùbá phrase *Kiri yó*. This is folk-etymology: seeking to find the meaning of obscure words within the confines of a single language. Historical comparative linguistics helps us to discover the meaning of such words by comparison with their cognates in related languages.

Historical Linguistics

Historical comparative linguistics (HCL) is the study of language change over time. Principle concerns of HCL include:

1. to describe and account for observed changes in particular languages
2. to reconstruct the pre-history of languages and to determine their relatedness, grouping them into language families (comparative linguistics)
3. to develop general theories about how and why language changes
4. to describe the history of speech communities
5. to study the history of words, i.e. etymology

The principle method of historical linguistics is the *Comparative method*: A method of reconstruction in historical linguistics based on comparison of cognate forms in related languages. A cognate can be defined as such:

- **cognate**: A word (or morpheme) that is related to a word (morpheme) in sister languages by reason of these words (morphemes) having been inherited by the related languages from a common word (morpheme) of the proto-language from which they descend. For example, Italian *cane* /kane/, Portuguese *cão* /kãũ/, French *chien* /šyɛ̃/ 'dog', are all cognates, since they descend in these Romance languages from the same original word in Latin (ancestor of the Romance languages): *canis* 'dog'.
- **cognate set:** A set of cognate words (morphemes), a set of words related to one another in the sister languages because they are inherited and descend from a single word (morpheme) of the proto-language.[8]

The comparative method (CM), like the scientific method of the natural sciences, has a set of procedures aimed at falsifying hypotheses, eliminating chance and human biases. The steps in the CM are listed as follows:

- **Step 1: Assemble cognates**
  Step 2: Establish sound correspondences
- Step 3: Reconstruct the proto-sound
  Step 4: Determine the status of similar (partially overlapping) correspondence sets
- Step 5: Check the plausibility of the reconstructed sound from the perspective of the overall phonological

8 Lyle Campbell & Mauricio J. Mixco, *A Glossary of Historical Linguistics*, (Edinburgh: Edinburgh University Press), 2007, pp. 33-34.

inventory of the proto-language
- Step 6: Check the plausibility of the reconstructed sound from the perspective of linguistic universals and typological expectations
- Step 7: Reconstruct individual morphemes

As stated previously, the CM is used to falsify hypotheses and this is echoed by Michael Weiss in his article "The Comparative Method."[9]

> The first step in applying CM is formulating a hypothesis that the given languages to be compared are in fact descended from a common source. It obviously makes little sense to apply the Comparative Method to languages that evidently aren't related – at any reasonable time depth – and the failure of the procedure to reveal any regularity of correspondence would be a strong argument against a theory of genetic common origin. **Thus, the Comparative Method, strictly speaking, is not a method for generating relationship hypotheses, but rather is a crucial tool for either confirming or not confirming such hypotheses**. (Bowern & Evans, 2014: 128) (bolded emphasis mine)

While the details of how the comparative method works in full is beyond the scope of this essay, a small example will help the reader understand, to some degree, all that is involved in the process.

The following example comes from the Minahasan group of languages, which are spoken in the North Celebes, Indonesia, and part of the Western Malayo-Polynesian branch of the Austronesian phylum. The word under examination has the meaning of "fence, enclosure." We can see how the words compare in the related languages listed to the left.[10]

[fence, enclosure]			1	2	3	4	5	
Tondano. *paɣər*	≡	Φ_{χ}(	p	a	ɣ	ə	r	)
Tonsea. *pagər*	≡	Φ_{λ}(	p	a	g	ə	r	)
Tombula. *pagər*	≡	Φ_{μ}(	p	a	g	ə	r	)
Tontemboan. *pagər*	≡	Φ_{ν}(	p	a	g	ə	r	)
			↓	↓	↓	↓	↓	
P.Minahasan	≡	*	p	a	g	ə	r	

As we can see here, all of the phonemes correspond neatly with each other in related languages. We reconstruct Proto-Minahasan **pagər* "fence, enclosure" based on the principle that the forms of each phoneme that dominates within a correspondence set is chosen as the ancestral phoneme to explain its presence in the daughter languages. For example, out of the *ɣ, g, g, g* series above, we reconstruct [*g] because it has the most representations in the median position in the series.[11] All reconstructions are theories on the relationship between shared characteristics (in phonology, morphology, semantics, grammar) in related languages. In other words, they are explanations for a series of thoroughly tested and confirmed observations. We can apply this method in confirming or discovering etymologies. We will conduct a small case-study using the Egyptian and Yorùbá languages below.

The word *ẖsj* [Wb 3, 398-399.10; FCD 204] in the Egyptological literature is defined as "weak, feeble, cowardly, humble (of rank), mean (of conduct), vile (of enemies, speech), wretched, coward." At times, the Egyptians used this term to refer to their foreign enemies, especially the Nubians to the south. Early Egyptologists attempted to argue that this term was in fact a 'racial' term to negatively refer to the 'blacks' as opposed to the Egyptians, who in their minds, were 'white'. To discover whether this word had any racial

9 Claire Bowern and Bethwyn Evans (Eds.), *Routledge Handbook of Historical Linguistics*, (London: Routledge), 2014, pp. 127-145.

10 From J.N. Sneddon, *Proto-Minahasan: Phonology, Morphology and Wordlist*, (Canbera: Australian National University), 1978.

11 Actual practice would be a bit more involved. But we are keeping it simple to facilitate discussion without writing an entire text on HCL.

connotations requires a philological approach. But to ascertain the meaning of the term requires an HCL approach that would supplement the data obtained from the philological analysis.

The first step in our analysis is to establish the sound-meaning correspondences between two potential cognate sets. To keep it simple we will do this with just two languages: ciKam and Yorùbá.

Table 1: Comparative table between ciKam and Yorùbá

ciKam	Yorùbá	Correspondences
ssm.t "horse"; *smsm* "horse" (obsolete)]	*ẹṣin*, "horse"	s- : ṣ- -m : -n
zn "to open"	*ṣí* "to open"	z- : ṣ- -n : -ø
zš "to open"		
zj "to go"	*ṣiṣẹ́* "to work" *ṣíṣẹ* "to labor, to worry"	z- : ṣ-
zf "to cut up; to slaughter" *zwꜣ* "to cut (down, off); to break"	*ṣá* "to cut; to wound with a knife"; *aṣá* "a heavy spear or javelin used to kill elephants" (with noun forming prefix *a-*); *oṣe* "club of god of thunder [*Ṣango*]" (a striking instrument);	z- : ṣ- -f : -ø
wsi "to saw, cut up, trim"		
ḥzy "a body of water"	*ṣìn* "to wash; to rinse"	ḥ- : ø- -z- : -ṣ- -y : -ì -ø : -n
ḥzmn "to cleanse; to purify"		

From the table above we can see that Egyptian *z/s* regularly corresponds to Yorùbá *ṣ* [ʃ] /sh/. We also notice that the sounds represented by the Egyptian graphemes /ḥ/ and /w/ are absent in Yorùbá. A matter of fact, any *h*-type sounds in related languages are absent in Yorùbá comparative studies (Oduyoye 1996). The Egyptian sound represented by *ꜣ* [ʀ̃] is also absent from Yorùbá, as the following table confirms:

Table 2:

ciKam	Yorùbá	Correspondences
wꜣs "fortunate, prosperous, well-being, prosperity"	*àṣẹ* "the force to make all things happen and multiply" (Thompson, 1984:18) [Pulaar *waas* "riches" (Lam, 1994: 44)]	w- : ø- -ʀ̃- : -ø- -s : -ṣ
	ajé "money, the goddess of money" (s > j)	w- : ø- -ʀ̃- : -ø- -s : -j
wꜣs "to batter, to strike, to break, to bruise, to lay" *wꜣs* "ruin"	*ọṣẹ́* "hurt, injury"; *ẹṣẹ́* "blow with the fist";	w- : ø- -ʀ̃- : -ø- -s : -ṣ

wꜣs "scepter" 	*àṣẹ* "scepter"	w- : ø- -R̃- : -ø- -s : -ṣ
wꜣs "dominion, have dominion, power"	*àṣẹ* "authority, power, law, command"	w- : ø- -R̃- : -ø- -s : -ṣ
wꜣs "honor (due to a god or king), prestige"	*ọ̀ṣọ́* "elegance, finery, neatness, jewels" *ọzō* **(Igbo)** "honor, title of high degree" [Pulaar *wasu* "glorification" (Lam, 1994: 44)]	w- : ø- -R̃- : -ø- -s : -ṣ
	eze "to honor, to participate to assume a role of privilege"	w- : ø- -R̃- : -ø- -s : -z
siꜣ "recognize, to know, perception, knowledge" *siꜣ* "to notice, be aware of, insight, reason" (*ꜣ* = r/l)	*ṣé* "to see"	s- : ṣ- -j- : -ẹ́- -R̃ : -ø
zꜣ "to watch for" *zꜣ.w* "to guard; to heed; to guard against"	*ṣọ́* "to watch"	s- : ṣ- -R̃ : -ø
sjꜣ.tj "leg (of Osiris) (a relic)"	*ẹsẹ̀* "leg; foot"	s- : s- -j- : ẹ̀ -R̃ : -ø

Now that we have established the sound meaning correspondences, we can establish the cognate for M-E (Middle-Egyptian) *ẖsj* "wretched."[12] Further comparative analyses confirm that the root of *ẖsj* is *-s-*, which can be found in the Yorùbá language as the word *ṣẹ̀* "to offend" and *ṣì* "to miss." The Yorùbá word *ẹ̀ṣẹ̀* "sin" is cognate with the Hebrew/Arabic word for "to sin" (< "to miss"): *ḥaṭa*. The *-ṣ-* in Yorùbá *ṣi/ẹṣi* and *ẹṣẹ* corresponds to the *-t-* in Hebrew *hata'*. The initial *h-* drops in Yorùbá. For a cross check we can examine two other Yorùbá words: *ọ̀ṣì* "wretchedness" and *ìṣẹ̀* "property." They correspond with a homonym of Hebrew *hata'*, which means "penury" ("poverty, indigence, neediness, pennilessness"). Historically the Yorùbá thought of *ẹ̀ṣẹ̀* "sin" as they thought of *àṣiṣe* (*à-ṣì-ṣe*) "a mistaken deed, a deed that is wide of the mark" (< *ṣì/ṣè; èṣì* "an unprecedented mistake, an accidental error"; *ṣiṣì* "missed; mistaken"; *ṣiṣe* "to misbehave"). Compare with *ṣìṣọ* "to speak wrongly; to make a slip of the tongue"; *ṣọ̀ṣi* "to be wretched." The Yorùbá language provides a wide range of concepts for this root that provide context for our Egyptian term.

Thus, if our comparison is sound, we can make the argument that essentially M-E *ẖsj* is a word with a fundamental meaning of "sin" or "to go off path; miss the mark."[13] Its cognate in the Yorùbá language is: *ọ̀ṣì* "wretchedness"; *ṣọ̀ṣi* "to be wretched." An additional cognate for the Yorùbá terms in ciKam is *wꜣs* "a miserable person; wretch" [Wb 1, 261.8] given the many *wꜣs* correspondences in Table 2. This would perfectly explain why the term was first used in the Egyptian literature, in a political sense, to refer to the Egyptians themselves; as discussed in Mario Beatty's essay "Xsy "Wretched": The Anatomy of a Foreign Relations

12 *Wretch* "an unfortunate or unhappy person" > "wretched "(of a person) in a very unhappy or unfortunate state; of poor quality; very bad; used to express anger or annoyance."

13 In middle Egyptian, a cognate—which is actually a doublet in the language (or a possible loan)— for the word *ẖsy* is the word: *thj* "go astray, attack (with), transgress, falsify, divert (pain), err, debauch, seduce, violate, mislead, **overstep (path),** disobey, impugn (one's character), falsify (account), rebel (against), neglect (appointed dates), reject (petitions), violate (corpse)." This is reflected in Yorùbá as /àìtò/ "that which is not straight forward" and /àìye/ "that which is not befitting, the unbecoming."

Concept."[14] When Ankhtifi of Mo'alla says, "On whomsoever I laid my hand—no harm could approach him, because my reasoning was so expert and my plans were so excellent. But every ignorant person, **every wretch who opposed me**, I retaliated against him for his deeds,"[15] it further confirms the meaning of *ẖsj* as someone who is "off path, misguided, misdirected" from the course laid out by a superior. In other words, *ẖsj* is opposed to *mꜣꜥ.t*, which is defined as having "walked the correct path" (Imhotep 2019).

When it comes to the word *km.t*, we have to go through the same process as above to establish the relevant sound-meaning correspondences required to do a proper etymology. But our process is going to be a little bit more intense. In addition, we note that we must account for all of the phonemes, the sounds, represented by the phonographs in the word *Km.t* 𓆎𓅓𓏏𓈇. However, we can start simply by examining the initial consonants in a series to see if we have grounds to compare the two languages. As noted by Hermel Hermstein in his *Black Sumer: The African Origins of Civilisation* (2012), concerning the process of eliminating chance from our correspondence set:

> It should be emphasised that COGNANCY is based on recurrent sound correspondences and not sound resemblance. We can illustrate this with the English word 'heart' which has an identical sound to the German word hart but this is a chance resemblance. Even though English and German are related this does not automatically make them COGNATES. We know it is a chance resemblance because the German hart is actually COGNATE with the English word 'hard'. We know they are COGNATE because the observed recurring sound correspondence of German 't' is with English 'd'. Recurrent sound correspondences are the only way to demonstrate genetic relationships between languages. They exclude chance resemblances. The linguistic researcher Fari Supiya has devised, what we shall call, the Repeat Initial Consonant Correspondence Test (RICCT) with a view to excluding chance by quick inspection of a word list. (Hermstein, 2012: 42)

But given that *Km.t*, it is assumed, contains a two-consonant root, then it is best to compare the two consonants simultaneously, which will further eliminate chance.

> ... Some languages are, however, are dominated by roots which have a consonant-vowel (CV) or consonant-vowel-consonant (CVC) structure. This means that finding a four-consonant paradigm in basic vocabulary, after the manner suggested by Nichols, would be almost impossible in a comparison of two CVC languages. There will be many two-consonant paradigms but not four-consonant paradigms. Such languages, however, tend to have a high number of HOMOPHONOUS roots, that is roots which have the same sounds but two or more unconnected meanings. **If a CVC root with the exact same two unconnected meanings is found in a second language, with recurring sound correspondences, then this is a four-consonant paradigm.** This kind of evidence is PROBATIVE or individual-identifying because it is very unlikely to occur by chance. It is also very unlikely that a CVC root's two unconnected meanings of basic vocabulary would *both* be BORROWED by another language. In this way the Repeated Two-Consonant Paradigm (RTCP) was devised by the present author, having been inspired by the work of Nichols. (Hermstein, 2012: 46) (bolded emphasis mine)

While he may believe he originated the repeated two-consonant paradigm, other scholars (including myself) have been utilizing this technique independent of Hermstein. One such scholar is Frank Kammerzell. In his article "Old Egyptian and Pre-Old Egyptian: Tracing Linguistic Diversity in Archaic Egypt and the Creation of the Egyptian Language," Kammerzell provides us with some important conditions for justifying historical relations between two linguistic systems. We can argue that two or more languages are related when:

- There are not only roots or word stems which are similar in shape and meaning, but both systems also exhibit similar sets of stem extensions and/or derivative affixes used on the same basis.
- Particular lexemes exhibit formally similar suppletive stems[16] in both systems.

14 In: *Ankh* n°17, 2008, pp. 30-39.

15 Ian Shaw (Ed.), *The Oxford History of Ancient Egypt*, (Oxford: Oxford University Press), 2000, p. 120.

16 In linguistics and etymology, *suppletion* is the replacement of one stem with another, resulting in an allomorph of a morpheme which has no phonological similarity to the other allomorphs. Stated a different way, it can be understood as the use

- In either system there are similar groups of semantically distinct lexemes which share the same phonological shape or matching groups of phonologically distinct lexemes having the same meaning. So, e.g., roots of the consonantal shape ***ml**- serve to express the semantic concepts **'black', 'sing',** and **'weak'** in Indo-European as well as in Egyptian. Since there is no apparent universal conceptual resemblance between 'black', 'sing', and 'weak', the probability that two distinct languages denote these meanings by means of the same root independently from each other is extremely small. (Kammerzell, 2001: 218).

On the latter point, what Kammerzell is essentially saying is that, in the case of Indo-European, it is highly unlikely that a set of languages would, by accident, have a series of words with the *m-l* consonant sequence with the meanings "black," "sing," and "weak." The presence of such a series is a strong indicator of a relationship. We show this methodology with a two-consonant paradigm between Proto-Bantu, Sumerian, and ciKam (Egyptian) in Table 3 below.

Table 3: Proto-Bantu *-ng* and ciKam *-ꜣ* in C_2 (Formula *-ʀ̃ŭ or *-ʀ̃ĭ)

Proto-Bantu	Sumerian	ciKam	Correspondences
*-*tanga* "mat; sail"	*šar* "cloth designation"	*ṯꜣ.w.t* "sail" [*ṯꜣ.y.t* "fabric; mummy bindings; sail; curtain"[NK]]	t̠- : š- : t̠- -ng : -r : -ꜣ
*-*tUnga* "basket"	*šu* "basket"	*ṯꜣ.y* "a receptacle" (box, basket)	t̠- : š- : t̠- -ng : -ø : -ꜣ
*-*tUng*- "plait; sew; build"	*tug* "textile"	*tꜣ.j.tjt* "tissue; fabric; textiles" *tꜣ.j.t* "Tait (a weavers' town in Lower Egypt)" *tꜣ.w* "God's clothes"	t- : t- : t-, -ng : -g : -ꜣ
*-*tangu* "house, ground, wall"	*sig* "place" *zig* "town, center"	*tꜣ* "land; earth, ground, country"	t- : s- : t-, -ng : -g : -ꜣ
*-*tángúá* "sun"	*šeĝ* "to cook; to dry a field; to fire (pottery)"	*tꜣ* "being hot; burn"; "kiln"	t- : š- : t-, -ng : -ĝ : -ꜣ
*-*táng*- "to be first, be in front"	*saĝ* "front side" [*saĝ.ki* "forehead, brow, front"]	*šꜣ*ᶜ "begin, start, be the first, spring, originate, to elapse"	t- : s- : š- -ng : -ĝ : -ꜣ

The correspondences between all three languages are regular. It provides us with strong evidence of a possible relationship. But much more work would have to be done and we'd have to account for all of the irregularities in the data that is sure to arise as one phoneme in Language A, for example, may correspond to several phonemes in Language B. When this occurs, we must keep in mind the principle of *transitivity*.

Transitivity

In mathematics, a binary relation R over a set X is transitive if whenever an element *a* is related to an element *b* and *b* is related to an element *c*, then *a* is also related to *c*. A simpler way to say it would be:

If A → B, and B → C, then A → C.

---

of one word as the inflected form of another word when the two words are no cognate (the occurrence of an unrelated form to fill a gap in a conjugation (e.g., *went* as the past tense of *go*)). A suppletive series example can be seen in the English forms: *good, better, best*. In German, these forms are given as *gut, besser, besten*; Dutch *goed, beter, best*. Thus, a good case for a relationship between two languages is to see if they have suppletive stems as we see above that can only be argued as deriving from a common ancestor.

We highlight this fact because when one compares lexemes from Language A with lexemes from language B, a phoneme in language A may correspond to several phonemes in Language B, and vice-versa. The following tables are illustrative of this point. Here we compare lexemes from ciKam (Egyptian) with the modern Yorùbá language of Nigeria.

Table 4: *t-n* correspondences between ciKam and Yorùbá

ciKam	Yorùbá	Correspondences
***jtn**.w* "obscurities; riddles"	***ìtàn** lásán* "myth" (< *ìtàn* "story; narration; tale")	j- : i- -t- : -t- -n : -n
jtn "light"	*itanna* "lamp; flowers (so-called for their brilliancy)"	j- : i- -t- : -t- -n : -n
jtn "to shine; to illuminate"	***tan*** "to light a lamp or torch; to shine; radiate; entice; seduce; lure; deceive, spread; scatter" ***ìtan*** "a being related, to be related; spreading" ***itanu*** "the act of casting away; a casting off"	j- : i- -t- : -t- -n : -n
jtn "resting place; perch"	***itan*** "thigh; lap"	j- : i- -t- : -t- -n : -n
tm "to be complete"	***tán*** "finished; to finish, cease, extinct, be at the end, annihilate; to heal; cure"	t- : t- -m : -n
***tm**tm* "crusher"	***tàn**tàn* "violently"	t- : t- -m : -n
***tm**ꜣ* "mat" (gen.)	*à**tin*** "a soft mat which can be folded"	t- : t- -m- : -n- -ꜣ : -ø

As we can see from Table 4 above, Yorùbá *t-* corresponds regularly to ciKam *t-*. However, Yorùbá *-n* corresponds to both ciKam *-n* and *-m*. As we continue our experiment, we see that the same Yorùbá *t-n* consonant sequence also corresponds to *ḥ-m* in ciKam.

Table 5: ciKam *ḥ-m* correspondences with Yorùbá *t-n*

ciKam	**Yorùbá**	**Correspondences**
w.ḥm "further; again"; "to repeat"	***tún*** "again; once more"	ḥ- : t- -m : -n
ḥm "verb associated with curing an illness"	***tán*** "to heal; cure"	ḥ- : t- -m : -n
ḥm "to tread"	***tọnà*** "to follow the road; trace the path"; *i**tọna*** "a going in a way or path"	ḥ- : t- -m : -n
ḥm.y "helmsman" *ḥm.yt* "steering oar"	***tọnà*** "to take the lead, guide"	ḥ- : t- -m : -n

ḥw "driver, slugger, shepherd"		ḥ- : t- -w : -n
ḥmḥm "a jug (for milk and wine)"	***ọ̀tùn*** "a small pitcher or mug used for keeping holy water at a shrine"	ḥ- : t- -m : -n
ḥm "coward"	***ìtẹni*** "disgrace; a failure"	ḥ- : t- -m : -n
ḥwj "to strike; to blow"	***atọ́ni*** "provoker, aggressor";	ḥ- : t- -w : -n
ḥw "utterance"	***tẹnu*** "from the mouth"	ḥ- : t- -w : -n
	ìtumọ "meaning; explanations, elucidation, illustration, interpretation, comment" ***atúmọ̀*** "commentator; expositor"	ḥ- : t- -m : -m
ḥm "drive back; repel"	***tanù*** "to cast out; to eject"	ḥ- : t- -m : -n

Provided the above, we see that Yorùbá *-n* and *-m* correspond to ciKam *-w* as well. But this may be a unique case. In ciKam, when the voiced labials are in the intervocalic position (i.e., V_V), they often become [w] in the process. We write this formula as, for example, [m > w /V_V]. In the last table of this series, we can see that *ḥ-n* of ciKam also corresponds to *t-n* in Yorùbá.

Table 6: ciKam *ḥ-n* and Yorùbá *t-n* correspondences.

ciKam	Yorùbá	Correspondences
ḥn "to be fresh; to provide with"	***ọ̀tun*** "newness, freshness; novelty; new; fresh; recent"	ḥ- : t- -n : -n
ḥn.w "jar; chattel(s)"	***ọ̀tùn*** "a small pitcher or mug used for keeping holy water at a shrine"	ḥ- : t- -n : -n
ḥn "a protective container"		
ḥn.tj "ends; limits"	***tán*** "finished; to finish, cease, extinct, be at the end, annihilate; to heal; cure"	ḥ- : t- -n : -n
ḥn "a bad quality; greed"	***tẹ́ni*** "one who disgraces another"	ḥ- : t- -n : -n
ḥn "to hurry; pass by; retreat"; "to go speedily; to journey: to go"	***atọ̀na*** "one who walks about the road; a spy"	ḥ- : t- -n : -n
	ìtọna "a going in a way or path"	ḥ- : t- -n : -n
ḥn "to grow (of lotus)"	***tanná*** "to flower, to blossom"; ***itanna*** "blossom"	ḥ- : t- -n : -n
ḥn "to command; orders"	***tẹnu*** "from the mouth"	ḥ- : t- -n : -n

	ìtumọ "meaning; explanations, elucidation, illustration, interpretation, comment" *atúmọ̀* "commentator; expositor"	ḫ- : t- -m : -m

From the data in the tables, it appears as the ancestral phoneme for ciKam initial *t-* and *ḥ-*, and Yorùbá *t-* is [*k-]. The correspondences between ciLuba and ciKam confirms this.

Table 7:

ciKam	**ciLuba**	**Correspondences**
km "duty; profit"	*ntungù* "tip, reward, gratuity"	k- : t- -m : -ŋ
km.t "Egypt"	*di.tunga/ma.tunga* "country"	k- : t- -m : -ŋ
km.t  "grain or plant"	*di.tungù* "seed" (of corn, of millet)	k- : t- -m : -ŋ
km "put an end to"; *s.km* "to bring to an end; to finish out; spend"	*-tuuya* "to calm down; to diminish; to stop"	k- : t- -m : -ø

This type of correspondence often can be found in the reverse. In this case, ciKam *t-* will correspond to ciKam *k-*.

Table 8:

t-m	***k-m***	**Correspondences**
ḥ.tm "to destroy; to be destroyed"; "destruction"	*s.kmkm* "destruction"	t- : k- -m : -m
ḥ.tm "to pay (a debt)"	*km* "duty; profit"	t- : k- -m : -m
ḥ.tm "to provide with; to complete"	*km* "to complete"	t- : k- -m : -m
ḥ.tm "a mineral"	*km.w* "a substance (med.)"	t- : k- -m : -m

We notice here that there is an *ḥ-* prefix on the *t-m* roots in ciKam. That *t-m* is the root in *ḥtm* verified by ciKam *tm* "to cease; to perish"; ciLuba *-kàma* "stop; end; be settled (says of deal)"; ciKam *tmꜣ.t* [LP] "ancestress; mother"; ciLuba *nkambwà* "ancestor, grandfather, great-grandfather"; ciKam *tmm* "to close (a wound) (med.)"; ciLuba *-tunga* "to sew"; "slip on, pass a pointed stick through."

By understanding the principle of transitivity, as illustrated in the tables above, we can prepare to make more solid arguments concerning the etymology of words in a given language. This is the first step in establishing a Proof by Contradiction that we will discuss in the last section.

Derivation

If we assume that the word *Km.t* "Egypt" derives from a root *km* "black," and we want to cross check this assumption in related languages, we must first check to see if the word *km* "black" is not a secondary meaning from a more fundamental root in ciKam. In the ancient *r-n-km.t* (the Egyptian language), the color terms are actually derived from objects that personify that color or from verbs. The primary colors of Egypt are displayed in Table 9 below.

Table 9: Colors of ancient Egypt

	*dšr* "red"		*ḥḏ* "white"
	*dšr* "red"		*w3ḏw3ḏ* "grow green"
	*jrtjw* "blue"		*w3ḏ* "green"
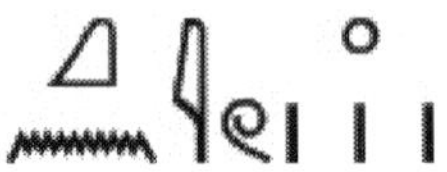	*ḳnjw*(*t*) "yellow"		*km* "black"

Each color pertains to some object in nature that displays that color. The words for colors derive from either nouns representing an object in nature, or a verb describing the action of a noun in nature. For example, the word *ḥḏ* "white" derives from a verb meaning "to shine, be bright" which explains the sun with sunrays [N8:] glyph as the terminating classifier. Reflexes of this term can be found in Yorùbá *ọ-jọ́* "day (light)"; Ilaje Yorùbá *ọ-jọ́* "sun (light)"; Yorùbá *a-jé* "cowrie" (white); Igala *Ọjọ́* "God"; Urhobo *ẹ-djọ* "divinities" (Adegbola, 1983: 353). It is from this root that we get the terms *w3ḏ.t* "Wadjet" (cobra goddess of Lower Egypt) [Wb 1, 268.17; LGG II, 269 ff.; LÄ VI, 906 ff.] < *ḏ.t* "viper, cobra" [Wb 5, 503.1-8; LÄ V 646; vgl. ONB 213] (Cf. Yorùbá *ejo* "snake"); for in African languages there is a correlation between "brightness, shining" and words for "snakes" (see Imhotep 2019).[17]

In the case of the word *km* "black," I argue here that it derives from a word for "hair" (more details in Imhotep 2019). Evidence can be gleamed from the following personal names:

 *bb-**km*** "PN/?" (RPN I 95.10)

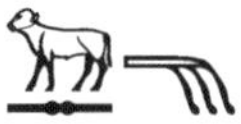 *bḥz-**km*** "PN/?" (RPN I 98.5)

As we can see here, the D3 hair glyph has the consonant sequence value of *km*, which helps to explain also why it is the classifier for *km* "black." The *km* form, in one dialect, became *šn* "hair." The form *km* may be a borrowing into M-E.

The above exercise is important because if we are going to do a comparative analysis on the word *km* "black" with other related languages, we do not first compare *km* "black" but **km* "hair" because the semanteme "black" is a derived form and not a primary meaning. A look into Sumerian will help us to find clarity.

Table 10 below shows the semantax by which the Sumerian words for black are derived. As we can see, both words for black in Sumerian derive from words for "tree" which has very dark colored wood.

---

17 For example, Yorùbá *i-go* "glass" (shining), Ngamba *ko* "eye," Igbo *e-gho* "cowrie shell money" (shining); *e-ke* "python" (< *ke* "shine"); Hausa *ga* "look at" (Adegbola, 1983: 377). Cf. Yorùbá *dán* [dã] "shine, dazzle," *didan* "shine, glisten," *edun* "white colobus monkey" (totem of twins); Fon *Dã* "the snake spirit, the guardian spirit" (*Dã* revealing himself as a snake); Ijo *odum* "python"; ciKam (NK) *dm* "worm"; Swahili *duma* "cheetah"; Igbo/Bini *odum* "lion" (powerful tawny animal). See also Hebrew *nehoš-ɛt* "bronze," *nahaš* "serpent." All terms derive from a more fundamental root meaning "to go" or "to propagate forward."

Table 10: Sumerian Semantax: tree → black

^{ĝeš}esi	"a tree"		
^{ĝeš}eš^{22}	"a tree; a terebinth; almond (tree)"		
^{ĝeš}gig	"a tree; a resin"	giggi; gi^{6}-gi^{6}	"(to be) black"
^{ĝeš}mes	"a tree"	mes; ^{ĝeš}mes	"blackness, black spot; black wood"
^{ĝeš}maš	"a tree"		
ĝeš; mu; u^{5}	"tree; wood; a description of animals"		

Note that *š* ~ *s* in Sumerian interchange. Also, *ĝ* ~ *m*: (ĝ = [ŋ]) interchange. Thus, *ĝeš* and *maš/mes* are dialectical variants of the same word. These forms are cognate with M-E *ẖ.t* "tree" [Wb 3, 339.10-341.11].[18] While *ĝeš* and *ẖ.t* "tree" are cognates in ciKam, *ẖ.t* does not lead to a word meaning "black." Thus, on this point, Sumerian and ciKam do not share the same semantax. This has to be done for every language where one is comparing M-E *km* "black" to a word "black" in some other language. If you find a word for "black" that you think is cognate with M-E *km* "black," but in that language it does not have a word for "hair" in a similar form as the word for "black" in that language, then more than likely these terms are not cognate and we have a case of a chance look-a-like.

Cheikh Anta Diop (1977: 92), for example, argues that Wolof *hem* "charcoal" and *hemb* "stoke the fire; fan the flames" is cognate with M-E *km* "black." Diop is under the impression that *km* "black" derives from a word #*km* "charcoal" or "fire" and this is clearly not the case. This is a chance look-a-like and so are all of the compared forms in Obenga (1992: 120).[19] The word for "black" in Wolof is *ñuul*. To their credit, they are essentially going off the WB entry *km* "pile of burning coals; kiln" [Wb 5, 122.10], but this form is not attested anywhere. This may be a ghost entry. From the evidence provided here (and in Imhotep 2019), the form *km* "black; to be black" is an innovation in ciKam.

Comparison of Morphemes

A morpheme is a meaningful morphological unit of a language that cannot be further divided (e.g. *in, come, -ing*, forming *incoming*). When we are doing comparative work, we must account for each morpheme in a word in the related languages. This will help to make our case of relatedness stronger and it further eliminates chance from our correspondence sets. In the case of Km.t, we assume that there are two morphemes: a root *km* + a *-t* suffix. It is believed that the *-t* suffix is a 'feminine' suffix. In Imhotep (2019), I challenge this notion and put forth another hypothesis to be tested. I argue that the *-t* suffix here is a morpheme for "place."

Early Egyptologists assumed that most words ending in *-t* displayed a gender suffix of the feminine. However, more researchers are realizing that there are more *-t* suffixes that are not the feminine *-t* and serve other purposes. One *-t* suffix is a place-name suffix and this is recognized by Julien Cooper in his 2015 dissertation *Toponymy on the Periphery: Placenames of the Eastern Desert, Red Sea, and South Sinai in Egyptian Documents from the Early Dynastic until the end of the New Kingdom.* The following examples reinforce this point.

18 All sound laws are verified in Imhotep (2019).

19 He compares M-E *km* with *i-kama* "to go black," "to blacken"; Bambara (Mali) *kami* "to reduce to embers"; Mossi (Burkina Faso); Vai (Liberia) *kembu* "black coal"; and Yaaku *kumpu* "black."

118		*Bpsti*	*/bbsti:/

Etymology (III): There is no phoneme /p/ in languages of this region, so the second consonant must mask an /f/ or /b/. If it is in the Beja area, one might think of the verbs *bubos* 'to cause to light up' or *baabis* 'bury in several graves' with the auslaut *-t* being a productive suffix in Beja toponymy.[20]

80		*Wkm.t*

A connection with the root *wgm* 'to grind, powder' makes sense, as this word is used in one text with *ḳm.yt* 'gum', the only known product of *Wkm.t*, but examples of a shift of *k* > *g* remains elusive in Middle Egyptian.[21] The connection with the root *wkm* giving the sense of 'to provide' might be the preferable option. The auslaut *–t* is easily explained as a *nomen loci*, 'providing(-place)' or a more abstract meaning, 'the-providing-one'.

60		*ḥrr.wt(y)* *t*

The placename *ḥrr.wt(y)t* [60] also contains a nominal suffix ***–t***, which might be analysed as being a collective suffix or as a *nomen loci* attached to a nominal root. (Cooper, 2015: 352)

69		*ṯnht*	*/cnht/ ~*/ t͡snht/

A difficulty with this connection is accounting for the auslaut *-t*, which must be a suffix, possibly a feminine marker.[22] In ancient Levantine toponymy, the suffix *-t* is witnessed in toponyms, but its exact morphological role is not apparent. Rainey suggests it may be a nominal or adjectival marker.[23] (Cooper,2015: 214)

More examples is given in Imhotep (2019) of this feature in Egyptian toponyms. The point here is that the presence of the *-t* suffix may indicate a place feature that lets the reader know the toponym is a name of a location (i.e., a place). This is very important because if this is indeed the case, then a reading of *Km.t* "the Blacks," as Diop (1977) has read it, is impossible given that the name refers only to a place and doesn't describe a people.

There is a particular methodology involved in studying toponyms. Paul Rahkonen, in his *A Study on Some Semitic Toponymic Types of the Second Millennium BC in the Southern Levant*,"[24] argues that one should study toponynms utilizing the following linguistic methods:

1. *Lexicon*: Sometimes even within the same language, different words, typical of different dialects, are used in place names. Especially when studying closely related languages, it is important to note that different synonymic

20 1631: Cf. *kwibis* 'to hide' > *kwabasat* 'hiding place', Bechhaus-Gerst, *Afrikanistische Arbeitspapiere* 61, 153. (Cooper, 2015: 299).

21 Note 1311: Wb. 1, 377 and Wilson, *A Ptolemaic Lexikon*, 270. Could *k* have shifted to *g* in Egyptian roots when in the environment of w? For the complexities of Egyptian velars, see Peust, *Egyptian Phonology*, 107-114. (Cooper, 2015: 239).

22 Note 1170: A. Rainey, *Canaanite in the Amarna Tablets: A Linguistic analysis of the mixed dialect used by the scribes from Canaan* (Leiden, 1996), I, 148 remarks that the suffixes **–ātu/āti/āte/āta** also occur in 'many masculine nouns'. For the suffix more generally, see *Lipinksi, Semitic Languages: Outline of a comparative grammar*, 225, 243; Hoch, *Semitic Words*, 444. An Old Kingdom Semitic toponym *ann.t* might also reflect the same morphological suffix, although N. Kanawati & A. McFarlane, Deshasha: The Tombs of Inti, Shedu and Others (Sydney, 1993), pl. 26 record only *an*[n], unlike W. F. Petrie, *Deshasheh* (London, 1898), pl. 4 which has *an.t*. For this toponym, see also A.-L. Mourad, 'Siege Scenes of the Old Kingdom', BACE 22 (2011), 144. Better examples of this suffix occur in Old Kingdom Semitic toponyms from the Delta identified by Redford (*ʿnp.t, ʿnd.ty, Rḫt.t Nzꜣ.t*), **although it is difficult to know whether the -.*t* here is an Egyptian suffix or attributable to a Semitic morpheme**; see D. Redford, 'Some observations on the Northern and Northeastern Delta in the Late Predynastic Period', in Bryan & Lorton (eds), *Essays in Egyptology in honor of Hans Goedicke*, 201-210, 202-206.

23 Note 1171: A. Rainey, 'Toponymics in Eretz Israel', *BASOR* 231 (1978), 4 remarks that the suffix may be a sign of an '**earlier linguistic stratum**'. See also Elitzur, *Ancient Placenames in the Holy Land*, 227-228.

24 In: *Studia Orientalia Electronica, Volume 4* (2016), pp. 108–130.

words in toponyms may appear regularly, creating distinguishable limited areas of distribution…

2. *Phonetic characteristics*: … The phonetic history of old toponyms may reveal something of the original language behind the name or give some suggestions for dating. Rainey (Rainey & Notley 2006: 16) has proposed that the toponym ʾEdreʿî in Bashan and Naphtali (Num. 21:33; Josh. 19:37) should be derived from a language in which there was the phonetic development *ḏ > d (or ~ ḏ) in contrast to Hebrew and Phoenician *ḏ > z (Sivan 2001: 36). In that case, the word behind the name is, according to Rainey, 'arm', in this case 'branch of wadi' (with a toponymic prosthetic *aleph*; see section 6.4); cf. Arb. *ḏirāʿ*, Heb. *zĕroaʿ* 'arm'.
3. *Morphology*: For example, such toponyms as ʾEštaʾol and ʾEštəmoaʿ reveal that in the language behind the names, *ephtaʿol* (< *iphtaʿel*) verbal structure was found. This structure was non-existent in Biblical Hebrew, but existed in Moabite and probably in the Canaanite dialect that was spoken in the most southern parts of the Southern Levant. Rainey (Rainey & Notley 2006: 16) interprets it as belonging to an earlier stage of the language, but does not say which language (possible candidates might be Hebrew or Southern Canaanite).
4. *Structure of toponyms*: In different languages there are different structural ways to construct toponyms. For example, in some languages, the word for 'lake' is placed in front of the actual name, as in *Lago* Maggiore (Italian) and *Loch* Laomainn (~ Eng. *Lo*mond) In other languages, it is placed after the name, like Bad*en* See (German) or Stor|*sjön* (Swedish). Accordingly, in personal names the yahwistic theophoric elements were used as prefixes or suffixes in the Hebrew naming models during the Iron Age II (Golub 2014: 626). Suffixes are sometimes used to mark toponyms, as in the Finnish naming system with *-la* as the marker of settlements. (Gaelic). These kind of suffixal elements are called ***topoformants***. These morphemes serve as markers of toponyms. Most formants originate from so-called *generics* of names or from derivational affixes. A *generic* answers the question of the characteristics of a place: i.e., lake, river, village, mountain, hill, etc. (Rakhonen, 2016: 112-113)

It is structure of toponyms and the notion of *topoformants* that are instructive for our discourse. Some examples of topoformants can be seen below:

Great Britain:

Anglosaxon ****tun*** "enclosure, estate":	Ever|*ton*, Kings|*ton*.
Anglosaxon ****ham*** "farm":	Notting|*ham*, Burming|*ham*.
Anglosaxon ****burg*** > ***bury*** "fortification":	Sals|*bury*, Sud|*bury*.

Canaanite:

-ōn < **-ān* :	Sid|*ōn*, Ašqel|*ōn*.
bêṯ "house":	*Bêṯ*|Lehem
ʔayin > ***ʔên*** "spring":	*ʔEn*|Geb
may(im) > ***mê*** "water":	*Mê*|Neptoah

We argue in Imhotep (2019) that Km.t is an example of a *topoformant* and that the *-t* is a suffix for "land" and is derived from the word *tꜣ* "land; country." It is no different than saying Yorùbá-*land*, Igbo-*land*, etc. One must be aware of this type of information when engaging the argument on the meaning of Km.t as this is one of the details that has to be falsified. It should be noted that because of the homographic nature of the various suffixal *-t*'s in ciKam, that there was often much confusion by the scribes on how to handle this matter. As noted by Mboli (2010: 372):

> Les classes et les genres ont donc tendance à fusionner en M-E, devenant de plus en plus rares. À la fin, la seule distinction de classe qu'on peut déceler dans les six langues est celle qui existe entre les animés et les inanimés. En sango, le genre féminin et la classe des abstraits et des collectifs ont également fusionné et cette situation a dû remonter au tout dernier état du négro-égyptien. En effet ces trois catégories (féminin, collectif et abstraits) sont mentalement pensées comme liées les unes aux autres non seulement en M-E et en sango mais également en hausa et dans bien d'autres langues négro-africaines non traitées ici. Cet exemple montre comment la langue peut durablement agir sur la pensée au point de fusionnerdes concepts au départ très éloignés les uns des autres

[Classes and genders therefore tend to merge in M-E, becoming increasingly rare. In the end, the only class distinction that can be detected in the six languages is that between the *animate* and the *inanimate*. In Sango, the feminine gender and the class of abstracts and collectives also merged and this situation had to go back to the very last stage of Negro-Egyptian. Indeed, these three categories (feminine, collective and abstract) are mentally thought of as related to each other not only in M-E and Sango but also in Hausa and many other Black African languages not treated here. This example shows how language can have a lasting effect on thinking and merge concepts that are far apart from each other.]

The *-t* suffix in M-E represents the feminine, collective, and abstract. We add here that it also denotes a place. In fact, the abstract and place morphemes in Cyena-Ntu (Negro-Egyptian) are the same and derive from a root meaning "foot" > "place" > "abstract." This semantax survived in M-E as evidenced by *b/bw* "foot; place" > *bw* "place; prefix of the abstract" (e.g., *bw-mꜣꜥ* "accuracy; justice" [Wb 2, 14.12-19]). A complete analysis is done in Imhotep (2019).

Frequency of Use

Another thing a researcher has to consider in the argument of the meaning of Km.t, is the frequency of use of a given form. When one is trying to establish the grounds on which an argument is made for a given meaning, how many times a particular form is used informs us of how important this type of representation is to the people who use it. The more frequent its use, the more important it is to the people; and vice-versa.

A case in point, Diop's entire argument, that Km.t means "the black people," rests on the presence of a form of the word *km.t* [Wb 5, 127.20] with the seated man and woman classifiers. This version of the word Km.t can be found in the *Papyrus Kahun* of the XII Dynastic period. What readers may not realize is that, to my knowledge, this is the only source where this form of Km.t can be found. This is problematic for a number of reasons. The main reason is that it is statistically insignificant given its low frequency use.

While the *Thesaurus Linguae Aegyptae* (TLA) database does not contain the records of all Egyptian texts, it has a significant amount of texts stored that the frequencies of particular lexemes within its database can be meaningful for our discourse.[25] For example, Egypt was known by many names throughout its over 3000 year history. According to the TLA, the number one toponym, by frequency of use in the Egyptian texts present in its database, is *tꜣ.wj* "the two lands" (Egypt) [Wb 5, 217.1-219.3]. This word, in the Egyptian hieroglyphic database, has a frequency of 521 attestations at 5.17%.[26] The word *Km.t* "the black land" [Wb 5, 127.4-127.17] is only attested 293 times at 2.91%. This is telling for two reasons. Firstly, the number one reference to Egypt is a word that describes the physical landscape and simply is a word for "land." Secondly, the form of Km.t with the seated man and woman classifiers is only attested two, maybe three times in the Papyrus Kahun. Let's just assume that there is one other attestation in another papyrus somewhere, bringing our total to four. Out of the 293 attestations from the TLA, the form would only account for 1.4%[27] of the attested forms of the word. That means approximately 99% of the time the , , and forms were used. Each one of these forms utilize a classifier meaning a type of "land," which is consistent with the usage of the word *tꜣ.wj* "Egypt" as the number one toponym for the state. So why would Diop attempt to make such a strong argument based on a form with such a low frequency? At this frequency, it can be argued that the Egyptians made a mistake in the Kahun hieratic papyrus; that this was in fact chance. The form of Km.t does not occur enough in the record for us to establish a pattern or trend in which to analyze its importance or context. The question then becomes, "On what grounds should this form , which is only attested in one source on two occasions, take precedence over all of the other forms (291 attestations in the TLA) where the classifiers, in all three other forms, are glyphs for irrigated land (i.e., → →)?" At this juncture, its value is undetermined at best.

25 As of October 2014, the TLA comprises about 1,400,000 text words.

26 The place-name *tꜣ-mrj* "Ägypten" (Wb 5, 223.1-224.9) (lemma-no. 169110) is only used 81 times; with a toponymic percentage rate of .80%.

27 4 / 293 = .0136. We then multiply .0136 x 100 = 1.4.

It should be noted, however, that during the Demotic stage of writing (650- BCE), the number one toponym for Egypt was Km(j) (< Km.t) as the table below shows (from TLA).

Table 11: Top 20 toponym frequency – TLA Demotic Text Database

lemma	**frequency**	**percent**
km(j) "Ägypten; Fruchtland, Teil von Ägypten" (Erichsen, Glossar 564) (lemma-no. 6581)	433	12.32
tꜢj=w-ḏj "Teudjoi" (P. Rylands 9, I 2 u. oft) (lemma-no. -10)	143	4.07
mn-nfr «Memphis" (Erichsen, Glossar 161) (lemma-no. 2438)	142	4.04
ḏmꜤ "Djeme" (Turin N 766, A 8) (lemma-no. 7751)	90	2.56
iwnw "Heliopolis" (Erichsen, Glossar 24) (lemma-no. 413)	89	2.53
ḫmnw "Hermopolis" (Erichsen, Glossar 360f.) (lemma-no. 4510)	79	2.25
jb "Elephantine" (Erichsen, Glossar 49) (lemma-no. 764)	75	2.13
ḥ.t-nn-nsw "Herakleopolis" (Erichsen, Glossar 220 und 285) (lemma-no. 3911)	74	2.11
ikš "Äthiope, Nubier; [als Gottesbeiname]" (Erichsen, Glossar 45) (lemma-no. 724)	73	2.08
gbḫ "Koptos" (Erichsen, Glossar 577f.) (lemma-no. 6766)	64	1.82
pr-iw-lḳ "Philae" (Graff. Philae 417, 1) (lemma-no. 1997)	54	1.54
rꜤ-ḳd "Rhakotis, Alexandria" (Erichsen, Glossar 242 und 551) (lemma-no. 3447)	52	1.48
šmꜤ(Ꜣ) "Oberägypten; oberägyptisch" (Erichsen, Glossar 509) (lemma-no. 6019)	47	1.34
ibt "Abydos" (Erichsen, Glossar 27) (lemma-no. 447)	47	1.34
tꜢ-ḳḥj "[bei Teudjoi]" (P. Rylands 9 passim) (lemma-no. 7035)	44	1.25
pr-iw-wꜤb "Abaton (von Philae)" (Graff. Philae 417, 1) (lemma-no. -521)	40	1.14
sjwḫ "Siut" (Erichsen, Glossar 408) (lemma-no. 5011)	40	1.14
rsṯꜢw "Rasetau, Nekropole" (Erichsen, Glossar 256) (lemma-no. 3583)	34	0.97
mdj "Medien; Meder, Perser, Soldat" (Erichsen, Glossar 185) (lemma-no. 2767)	33	0.94
pꜢ-tꜢ-nḥs "Nubierland, Nubien" (Setne 2, passim) (lemma-no. -2406)	32	0.91

One wonders why there is a near absence of the form *tꜢ.wj* "Egypt; the two lands" during the Demotic period? More investigation is needed here.

Logic and Linguistics

While linguistics utilizes scientific procedures to analyze and obtain data, it is not, in the strictest sense, a natural science (save for *Phonology*). Linguistics is more kin to mathematics and philosophy in that, like mathematics, it makes it arguments through logic and not experiments in the traditional sense. Mathematics is the study of anything that obeys the rules of logic, using the rules of logic (Cheng, 2015: 10). Logic, in turn, is the study of consequence. It can also be stated that logic is the study of what makes an argument[28] good or bad. A bad argument is one in which the conclusion does not follow from the premises. Thus, the conclusion

28 An argument is a set of statements, one of which is called the conclusion and the rest of which are called premises. An argument is said to be valid if the conclusion must be true whenever the premises are all true. An invalid argument is one where it is possible for all the premises to be true and the conclusion to be false.

is not a consequence of the premises. Logic aims to determine in which cases a conclusion is, or is not, a consequence of a set of premises.

While science has the scientific method, which utilizes experiments to falsify hypotheses, mathematics has the logical method where facts are deduced only using cold hard logic. Mathematics has two broad purposes:

1. To provide a language for making precise statements about concepts, and a system for making clear arguments about them.
2. To idealize concepts so that a diverse range of notions can be compared and studied simultaneously by focusing only on relevant features. (Cheng, 2015: 143)

Linguistics operates the same way, which is why we are finding more mathematical type formulas and representations of linguistic arguments through equations in the field of linguistics. As linguistics relies on logical arguments, it must make precise statements without being ambiguous. For example, we defined a morpheme earlier as a meaningful morphological unit of a language that cannot be further divided. But we can be more precise. We can restate the definition like so:

> A string of phonemes $\Phi(a_1, a_2, ..., a_n)$ is a morpheme, if and only if there exists an x such that 'x' is its meaning (possibly unknown). Formally, therefore, the morphemes are of general form $\Phi(a_1, a_2, ..., a_n) \equiv_{df}$ 'x'.

In computer science, we take advantage of *predicate logic* when analyzing linguistic arguments and it allows us to create formulas for linguistic concepts. A *predicate* is a verb phrase template that describes a property of objects, or a relationship among objects (e.g. integers, real numbers, sets, functions, etc.) represented by the variables. The sentences: 'The shirt Lakesha is wearing is maroon"; "The book cover is maroon"; "The car Snoop is driving is maroon" come from the template "is maroon" by placing an appropriate noun/noun phrase in front of it. The phrase "is maroon" is a predicate and it describes the property of being maroon. We often give predicates names. Any of the following can represent the predicate "is maroon": i.e., "is_maroon," "MAROON," or "μ" (Greek [m] pronounced "mu"). If we adopt the Greek symbol μ to mean the predicate "is maroon," then any sentence that asserts an object "is maroon" can be represented as "$\mu(x)$", where x represents an arbitrary object. $\mu(x)$ reads as "x is maroon". You commonly see this notation in mathematics as f(x) or g(x) read "f of x" or "g of x," respectively.

Likewise, the sentences "Mboli gives the book to Wudjau", "Iyafemi gives some fufu to Obadele", and "Treshawn gives a lecture to Ebony" are obtained by substituting an appropriate object for variables x, y, and z in the sentence "x gives y to z". The template "... gives ... to ..." is a predicate and it describes a relationship among three objects. This predicate can be represented by Give(x, y, z) or G(x, y, z), for example. The point here is that linguistic concepts can be represented as mathematical formulas, which are abstract representations of logical arguments. Therefore, there is a correlation between linguistics, mathematics, and logic.

Proofs

Lastly, the relationship between mathematics and linguistics allows us to utilize proofs in making absolute arguments. Mathematical truth is often revered because of *proof*. In mathematics, everything is rigorously proved. Once something has been proved, it cannot be refuted. Recall that math is not science in the sense that it is not evidence based, but logically based; meaning that our arguments are valid because they are logically sound and create no contradictions.

There are many types of proof in mathematics: e.g., proof by cases, deductive and inductive proofs, direct proof, and proof by contrapositive. For this discussion, we will highlight the *proof by contradiction*. However, before we start there, we introduce here the concept of *logical equivalency*. The two statements *P* and *Q* are logically equivalent provided *P* is true precisely when *Q* is true. That is, *P* and *Q* have the same truth value under any assignment of truth values to their atomic parts (Levin, 2016: 169). A discussion on truth tables is beyond the scope of this essay, but we place here an example of logically equivalent statements using truth or logic tables.

P	**Q**	**¬P ∨ Q**	**P→Q**
T	T	T	T
T	F	F	F
F	T	T	T
F	F	T	T

This says, essentially, that no matter what *P* and *Q* are, the statements ¬P ∨ Q (read "not-*P* or *Q*") and P → Q (read "*P* implies *Q*") either both are true or both false. These statements, therefore, are *logically equivalent*.

In logic, *proof by contradiction* is a form of proof that establishes the truth or validity of a proposition by first assuming that the opposite proposition is true, and then shows that such an assumption leads to a contradiction. Let us look at a linguistic case. We introduced earlier the concept of a *cognate* (words that share a common etymon). An example can be seen below with two words from different Indo-European languages:

$\Phi(a_1, a_2, ..., a_n) \equiv_{df}$ 'x' : $\Theta(b_1, b_2, ..., b_m) \equiv_{df}$ 'y'

Hittite. *guen·zi* ≡ 'kill·[3sg-pr]' : Rig-Veda. *han·ti* ≡ 'kill·[3sg-pr]'

The Hittite word *quen.zi* and the Rigveda *han.ti* "kill" are cognates because they descend, as proven through the comparative method, from the same common ancestor. In other words, these two terms are equivalent: they share the same truth value (i.e. "kill"). Using the comparative method, we can establish cognates within the same language, which would be evidence of dialects. To demonstrate the presence of dialects, it would be possible to conduct a two-consonant paradigm test on a series of lexemes that show regular sound-meaning correspondences. We will demonstrate such a case further down in our discussion. But first let's look at a comparison between ciKam and ciLuba concerning M-E √*mr*.

Table 12:

ciKam: *m-r*	ciLuba: *k-m*	Correspondences
mr.j "to love; to wish"	*-kàma* "to love; to desire, to wish; to think"	m- : -m -r : k-
	-kèma "wonder, wonder at, admire"	
mr.w "desert" *	*-kama* "dry up; evaporate"	m- : -m -r : k-
mr "weaving"	*-kùma* "spinning, making thread; make fabrics, weave"	m- : -m -r : k-
mr.t "divine songstress personified"	*ngìmbà* "singer, chanter, professional singer"	m- : -mb -r : g-
mr.t "black cow"	*ngombe*(a) "cow, beef, livestock"	m- : -mb -r : g-
mr.w "cedar"	*mu.kàmbà* ~ *mu.tàmbà* "beam; timber"	m- : -mb -r : k-
mr.j "pole"		
mr "partisan, supporter"		

ciKam: *m-r*	ciLuba: *k-b*	Correspondences
mr "bundle (of clothing)"	*di.kuba* "bundle, package, package, bundle"	m- : -b -r : k-
	di.bùki "bundle, parcel, bunch, package; baggage"	
mr "love"	*-kùba* "protect; take care of, make sure; monitor, observe"	m- : -b -r : k-

*[29]

As I discuss in Imhotep (2019), many two-consonant sequence roots, with the values CVCV or CVC, are often switched in related languages or dialects.[30] In this case here, M-E /m/ corresponds to ciLuba /m/, /mb/, and /b/. However, M-E /r/ corresponds to ciLuba /k/ and /g/. Not only that, the syllables are reversed in ciLuba in comparison to ciKam. Thus, *mr* in Egyptian is *rm* (< *km*) in ciLuba. We see the same type of correspondence between two dialects of ciKam. We observe the following:

Table 13:

ciKam *kweke*	ciKam *kekwe*	ciLuba	Correspondences
mr.j "to love; to wish"	-	*-kàma* "to love; to desire, to wish; to think" *	m- : ø : -m -r : ø : k-
mr.w "servants; underlings"	*km*  "service, duty, work"	-	m- : -m : ø -r : k- : ø
mr.tj "the two Meret goddesses" (uraes)	*km.y*  "snake, a 'black' desert cobra"	-	m- : -m : ø -r : k- : ø
mr.w "desert" **	-	*-kama* "dry up; evaporate"	m- : ø : -m -r : ø : k-
mr "weaving"	-	*-kùma* "spinning, making thread; make fabrics, weave"	m- : ø : -m -r : ø : k-
mr.t "divine songstress personified"	-	*ngìmbà* "singer, chanter, professional singer"	m- : ø : -mb -r : ø : g-
mr.t "black cow"	*km.t*  "(black) cow"	*ngombe*(a) "cow, beef, livestock"	m- : -m : -mb -r : k- : g-
mr.w "cedar"	-	*mu.kàmbà* ~ *mu.tàmbà* "beam; timber"	m- : ø : -mb -r : ø : k-
mr.j "pole"			
mr "partisan, supporter"			
mr "bundle (of clothing)"	-	*di.kuba* "bundle, package, package, bundle" ***	m- : ø : -b -r : ø : k-

29 *-w* place suffix.

30 For example, $\mathbf{C}_1V\mathbf{C}_2V$ in Language A → $\mathbf{C}_2V\mathbf{C}_1V$ in Language B.

mr.w "strips of cloth; bundle; bunch (as a measure of vegetables)"	*km* "black leather"	*nkanda* "skin, hide, peel, rind, bark, crust, covering, integument; a bundle of cloth done up in a skin; hence any bundle of cloth; leather, parchment, paper, book, epistle, letter, note, contract, engagement, document, register; "book""	m- : -m : -nd -r : k- : g-
-	*km.yt* "book of wisdom"	*mu.kanda* "book"; "paper"; "letter"	ø : -m : -nd ø : k- : k-
ḥm "chief"	*km-(wr)* "great power, bull, king"	*ngenda* "a title (of nobility), dignity, rank, degree"	-m : -m : -nd ḥ- : k- : g-
mr.ytj "ref. to crocodiles" ****	*km*  "crocodile's tail"?	*ngandu* "crocodile" *****	m- : -m : -nd -r : k- : g-

*[31] \| **[32] \| ***[33] \| ****[34] \| *****[35]

With the above tables establishing our cognates based on the 'sound laws', we are able to establish yet another internal cognate for the place name Km.t in the Egyptian language.

Table 14:

Glyph	***m-r***	**Glyph**	***k-m***
	*t3-mr.j* "Egypt" *		*km.t* "Egypt"
	*mr.t* "black cow" **		*km. t* "(black) bovines"
	*mr* "bull" ***		*km.t* "black" (the Serapeum"
	*mr-wr* "Mnevis" ****		*km-wr* "the great black one" (Osiris) *****
	*mr-wr* "lake Moeris" ******		*km-wr* "region of the Bitter Lakes" *******
-	*mr-wr* "the great black" (a snake) ********		*km.y* "snake, a 'black' desert cobra"

31 See also ciLuba: *-kèma* "wonder, wonder at, admire".
32 *-w* place suffix.
33 We also have the syllabic inverse *di.bùki* "bundle, parcel, bunch, package; baggage."
34 [Barta, Gespräch eines Mannes mit seinem Ba, 34, Anm. 59].
35 C.f. Bassa *n̄gaân* "crocodile"; Duala, Lingala *ngando*, CiLuba *ngandu* "crocodile."

*36 | **37 | ***38 | ****39 | *****40 | ******41 | *******42 | ********43

Given that *tꜣ-mrj* and *Km.t* are equivalent, and that *tꜣ-mrj* is not defined as "the black land," then Km.t cannot mean "the black land" either. We have just provided a proof by contradiction, which is based on the logical equivalency provided the establishment of cognates. In Chapter 3 of this volume, more cases of equivalents to Km.t will be provided. None of the other internal cognates of Km.t are defined as "the black land," and helps to demonstrate the error made by the early lexicographers. If Km.t means "the black land" or "the black people," then every instance of the dialectical variants (as shown in Chapter 3) need to be redefined with these meanings. We can do the same for *Km-wr* "Athribis." But let us establish some cognates first.

Table 15: *kꜣ* ~ *km* correspondences in ciKam

kꜣ "food, provisions"	*km.y*(*t*) "food"	k- : k- -ꜣ : -m
kꜣ "a material" (for vessels)	*km.t* "a jar"	k- : k- -ꜣ : -m
kꜣ "bull"	*km.y*  "(black) bull"	k- : k- -ꜣ : -m
	km.y "herd of cattle"	
kꜣ "bull snake" (i.e. a powerful serpent)	*kmy* "a snake"	k- : k- -ꜣ : -m
kꜣ "to appear" (syn. "look")	*km.t* "complete eye" (*-t* nominal suffix)	k- : k- -ꜣ : -m
kꜣ.wt "works"	*km* "perform, work"	k- : k- -ꜣ : -m
kꜣ.wj "worker"		
kꜣꜣ "a rock (quartz)"	*km.w* "a mineral"	k- : k- -ꜣ : -m

Provided the correspondences above, and the principle of transitivity, we know that the phrase *kꜣ-wr* "the big bull" [LGG VII, 253 f] and *km-wr*  "great black one (Osiris)" [Wb 5, 126.1-2; LGG VII, 284] are equivalent. We can cross check with the words *kꜣ-wr* "Great Serpent" [LGG VII, 254] and *km-wr* "The Great Black (a Serpent)" [LGG VII, 284]. The only reason why the Egyptologists interpret the word *km* in *km-wr* as "black" is because the word *km* "black" is a homograph. But if it meant "black," so would its cognate *kꜣ*. It should be interpreted simply as "bull" (or "snake" in the other reference) with no color connotation. This is not to say that the Egyptians didn't at times take advantage of the homography to imply some kind of relationship between the two terms (paronymy). But it is clear they understood they were not the same as the word *km.y* "bull" is never terminated (to my knowledge) with any color classifiers.

A few late period examples will show that the "black bull" and "Athribis" (*km-wr*) are two different things.

36 [Wb 5, 223.1-224.9].
37 [Wb 2, 106.10].
38 [Wb 2, 106.8; vgl. FCD 111].
39 [Wb 2, 106.4-6; LGG III, 328 f.].
40 [Wb 5, 126.1-2; LGG VII, 284].
41 [Montet, Gégraphie II 214 f.; LÄ II, 922 f.; vgl. alt Wb 2, 97.13 und GDG III, 50].
42 [Wb 5, 126.3-6; GDG I, 46, V, 202; Gomaà, Besiedlung II, 131; Wb 5, 125.12; GDG V, 200 f.; Gomaà, Besiedlung II, 148 ff.; GDG V, 203].
43 [LGG VII, 284].

Wsjr k3 km-wr ḥr jb km-wr
Osiris, the great black bull, who resides at Athribis (*km-wr*).[44]

Wsjr k3 km ḥr-jb km-wr
Osiris, the black bull, who resides at Athribis.[45]

As we can see here, the reason why *km-wr* "the great black" and *km-wr* "Athribis" are confused is because the Egyptians used these similar phrases together as a kind of play on words. In other words, paronymy is at use here. The black bull is *k3*. But as we can see, it has to be described as such using the word *km* "black." That the *km(y)* "bull" is not "the black bull" is evidenced by *mr* "bull" [Wb 2, 106.8; vgl. FCD 111], which has a variant *wr* "bull" [Wb 1, 331.12; LÄ V, 258]: *mr* > *wr* ; m > w /V__V. If *mr* were black, it would be defined as such.

We demonstrated that *k* ~ *g* interchange, especially during the Demotic period. We also note *m* and *n* interchange. Thus, we find *km* has dialectical variants as *gm* and *gn*. We argue here that *km-wr* "the great black" is actually a variant of the following:

gn-wr "the Great Ruler"[46]

Here the *k-* corresponds with *g-* and *-m* with *-n*. We have here *gn* "ruler" [Wb 5, 173.4], which is also defined as "be respected, be powerful" [Wb 5, 173.3]. Compare with the following:

gn-wr "a god who presided over offerings" (Budge 809a)

gm-wr [a variant of *gn wr* above]

The words *gn* and *gm* are dialectical variants of each other and mean the following:

---

44 Papyrus de *Ns-t3-nbt-išrw* : Budge, *The Greenfield Papyrus in the British Museum*, pl. 42; cite sous le sigle Ec; XXI dynastie. (Vernus, 1978: 292).

45 Papyrus d'Esoeris : Leemans, *Papyrus funeraire egyptien hieratique* (T 16), pl. XXX, LXXVI, 1.23; cite sous le sigle Leyde T 16; Epoque Ptolemaique. (Vernus, 1978: 293).

46 The phrase *gn-wr* can also be defined as "very distinguished" or "very respected" [LGG VII, 315; Pyr 2085c].

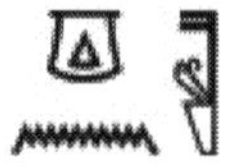

gn = powerful, respected

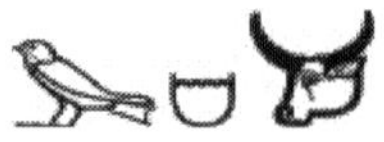

wr, kꜣ wr, hm wr "cow, ox, bull."

gn = bull

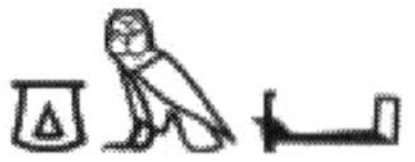

gm = strength, power, might

The word *gn* "bull" is a variant of *km* "bull, divine cattle" and both derive from a root meaning "power, be powerful." The bull is a metaphor for that which is big and strong and leaders along the Nile are known as "bull men." This is why I interpret *km wr* to mean "great power, great bull" and not "the great black" given the fact that there are no color classifiers given for this term. The word *km* "bull" to mean "power" can be seen in ciLuba *buKomu, ciKomu* "power," *nkama* "force, might, power, strength"; Kiswahili *ugumu* "strength, hardness, obstinacy"; Yorùbá *okun* "strength"; Kalenjiin *kiim* "firm, strong,"[47] *kiimnōt* "strength, power," *kimkim* "strong, stiff, firm, fundamental," *kiimnoteet* "strength, power." It is from this root that we get in ciBantu the word for "chief, king": e.g., ciLuba *wa-Kam, ci-komo* "chief," *mfumu* "chief"; Kikongo *mfumu* "chief"; Lingala *nkumu* "traditional religious chief"; Banda *kumu* "head, leader"; Zande *kumba* "husband"; Bambara *kũ* "head, leader." All are derived from C-N $*x^{w}u\eta^{w}u$ "chief." We note that in common Bantu *komo* (k-m) means "ox, cow" (Campbell-Dunn 2008: 109). Thus, we better understand the phrase *gn-wr* "the great ruler" and why *km-wr* should be interpreted in the same way: they are dialectical variants of each other. Therefore, *km-wr*  = "the great bull," "the great power," "the great ruler," "the most powerful."

Contemporary echoes of this theme are attested among the Nilotic-speaking culture of the Nyimang of the Nuba Hills, where the leader is a "Bull-Man."[48] Among the Cushitic-speaking culture of the Daasenеč of the Omo (East Africa), the political leaders of a generation are called *ara*, literally, "bulls" (Anselin, 2010: 48). We are reminded that Wjsr "Osiris" took on the identity of the *ḥp*  "Apis bull" [Wb 3, 70.1-4; LGG V 115 f.], which was previously associated with Ptah.

Conclusion

The aim of chapter was to introduce some of the problems one will encounter when trying to discover the etymology of the place-name Km.t; as well as the methods needed to solve them. As previously stated, a full analysis is forthcoming where many of these arguments are hashed out in great detail. Here we just wanted to empress on the mind of the reader some of the considerations that go into solving etymological and semantic problems. Provided that the etymology and meaning of the word *km.t* belongs to the domain of linguistics, it is only the tools of linguistics (such as the historical comparative method) that will help us discover the origin of the term and its real meaning in the text. A philological analysis alone will not bestow upon us that power. And philology alone will almost always lead to folk-etymology. Now that we understand these basics, we can move on to other aspects of the debate.

Selected Bibliography

ADEGBOLA, E.A. Ade. (Ed.). (1983). *Traditional Religion in West Africa*. Daystar Press. Ibadan, Nigeria.
ALLEN, James P. (2005). *The Ancient Egyptian Pyramid Texts*. Society of Biblical Literature. Atlanta, GA.
______ (2010). *Middle Egyptian: An Introduction into the Language and Culture of Hieroglyphs*, 2nd Edition.

47 *Kiim* can also mean "Insist, strengthen, emphasize a point."
48 See A. Kronenberg, "Notes on the Religion of the Nyimang." In: *Kush* 7, 1959, 197-213.

Cambridge University Press. Cambridge.
______ (2013). *The Ancient Egyptian Language: An Historical Study*. Cambridge University Press. Cambridge, New York, Melbourne, Madrid, Cape Town, Singapore, S˜ao Paulo, Delhi, Mexico City.

BEINS, Bernard C. and MCCARTHY, Maureen A. (2012). *Research Methods and Statistics*. Pearson Education, Inc. Boston, MA.

BENWARE, Wilbur A. (1998). *Workbook in Historical Phonology: Sound Change, Internal Reconstruction, Comparative Reconstruction*. University Press of America. Lanham, MD.

BOWERN, Claire and EVANS, Bethwyn (Eds.). (2014). *Routledge Handbook of Historical Linguistics*. Routledge. London.

BROMBERGER, Sylvain. (1992). *On What We Know We Don't Know: Explanation, Theory, Linguistics, and How Questions Shape Them*. University of Chicago Press. Chicago and London.

BRUGSCH, H-K. (1867-1882). *Hieroglyphisch-demotisches Wörterbuch*, Leipzig.

BUDGE, E.A. Wallis. (1904). *The Gods of the Egyptians: or Studies in Egyptian Mythology*. 2 vols. Open Court. London and Methuen and Chicago.

______ (1908). *The Book of the Kings of Egypt:Dynasties I-XIX*. Kegan Paul, Trench, Trubner & Co., Ltd., London.

______ (1925). *Egypt*. Williams & Norgate. London.

______ (2003). *Egyptian Hieroglyphic Dictionary, Vol.1 and II*. Kessinger Publishing, LLC. New York, NY.

BUNSUN, Margaret R. (2002). *Encyclopedia of Ancient Egypt*. Facts on File, Inc. New York, NY.

CAMPBELL, Lyle and MIXCO, Mauricio J. (2007). *A Glossary of Historical Linguistics*. Edinburgh University Press Ltd. Edinburgh.

CHAZAN, R., HALLO, W.W., and SCHIFFMAN, L.H. (1999). *Ki Baruch Hu: Ancient Near Eastern, Biblical, and Judaic Studies in Honor of Baruch A. Levine*. Eisenbrauns. Winona Lake, IN.

CHEN, Eugenia. (2015). *How to Bake π: An Edible Exploration of the Mathematics of Mathematics*. Basic Books. New York, NY.

CRESWELL, John W. (2009). *Research Design: Qualitative, Quantitative, and Mixed Methods Approaches*. Sage Publications. Thousands Oaks, CA.

CRUM, W.E. (1939). *Coptic Dictionary*, O.U.P. Oxford.

DIMMENDAAL, Gerrit J. (2011). *Historical Linguistics and the Comparative Study of African Languages*. John Benjamins Publishing Company. Philadelphia, PA.

DIOP, Chiekh A. (1991). *Civilization or Barbarism: An authentic anthropology*. Lawrence Hill Books. Brooklyn, NY.

______ (1974). *African Origin of Civilization: Myth or Reality*. Lawrence Hill & Co.

______ (1977). *Parenté génétique de l'égyptien pharaonique et des langue snégro-africaines: processus de sémitisation*. Les Nouvelles Éditions Africaines. Ifan-Dakar.

______ (1987). *Precolonial Black Africa: A Comparative Study of the Political and Social Systems of Europe and Black Africa, from Antiquity to the Formation of Modern States*. Lawrence Hill Company. Westport, CT.

______ (1989). *The Cultural Unity of Black Africa: The Domains of Patriarchy and Matriarchy in Classical Antiquity*. Karnak House. UK.

ERMAN, Adolph & Grapow, Hermann. (1971). *Wörterbuch der AegyptischenSpracheimAuftrage der deutschen Akademienhrsg Bd. I-V*. Unveränderter Nachdruck. Berlin.

FAULKNER, R.O. (1962). *A Concise Dictionary of Middle Egyptian*. Griffith Institute, Ashmolean Museum. Oxford

GARDINER. Alan H. (2007). *Egyptian Grammar: Being an Introduction to the Study of Hieroglyphs*, 3rd edition. Friffith Institute Oxford. Cambridge.

GOLDWASSER, Orly. (2002). *Prophets, Lovers and Giraffes: Wor(l)d Classification in Ancient Egypt*. Harrassowitz Verlag. Wiesbaden.

HANNING, Rainer. (1995). *Grosses Handworterbuch Agyptish-Deutsch : die Sprache der Pharaonen* (2800-950 v. Chr.). Verlag Philipp von Zabern. Mainz.

HERMSTEIN, Hermal. (2012). *Black Sumer: The African Origins of Civilisation*. Pomegranate Publishing. London.

IMHOTEP, Asar. (2014). "A Lesson in Egyptian Determinatives: The Case of KMT." Self-Published.

______ (2016). *Nsw.t Bjt.j (King) in Ancient Egyptian: A lesson in paronymy and leadership*. Madu-Ndela Press. Philadelphia, PA.

______ (2019). *Aaluja, Vol. II: Cyena-Ntu Religion and Philosophy*. Madu-Ndela Press. Philadelphia, PA.

KRUGER, Manfred G. and SCHLUTER, Julia. (Eds.). (2013). *Research Methods in Language Variation and Change*. Cambridge University Press. United Kingdom.

LAM, Aboubacry M. (1994). *Le Sahara ou La Vallee du Nil? Apercu sur la problematique du berceau de l'unite culturelle de l'Afrique Noire*. Editions MENAIBUC. France.

LURAGHI, Silvia and BUBENIK, Vit (Eds.), *The Continuum Companion to Historical Linguistics*. Continuum International Publishing Group. London | New York.

LEVIN, Oscar. (2016). *Discrete Mathematics: An Open Introduction*, 2nd Edition. Self-Published. CO.

LOPRIENO, Antonio. (1995). *Ancient Egyptian: A Linguistic Introduction*. Cambridge University Press. New York, NY.

LORD, Robert. (1966). *Teach Yourself Comparative Linguistics*. David Mackey Company, Inc. New York, NY.

LURAGHI, Silvia, and BUBENIK, Vit (Eds). (2010). *The Continuum Companion to Historical Linguistics*. Continuum International Publishing Group. London | New York.

MBOLI, Jean-Claude. (2010). *Origine des langues africaines: Essai d'application de la méthode comparative aux langues africaines anciennes et modernes*. L'Harmattan. Paris.

MCDOUGAL, Serie. (2014). *Research Methods in Africana Studies*. Peter Lang. NY | DC | MA.

MEEUSSEN, A.E. (1967), "Bantu Grammatical Reconstructions." In: *Africana Linguistica*, 3 (*), pp. 79-121.

MEILLET A. (1970). *La méthode comparative en linguistique historique*. H. Champion. Paris.

MENYUK, P. and BRISK, M. (2005). *Language Development and Education: Children With Varying Language Experiences*. Palgrave Macmillan. UK.

MOKHTAR, G. (Ed.). (1981). *General History of Africa, Vol II: Ancient Civilizations of Africa*. Heinemann | California | UNESCO.

MORRISON, W.M. (1906). *Grammar and Dictionary of the Buluba-Lulua Language: As Spoken in the Upper Kasai and Congo Basin.* American Tract Society. New York, NY.

NATIONAL Academy of Sciences. (2008). *Science, Evolution, and Creationism.* The National Academies Press. Washington, DC.

ODUYOYE, Modupe. (1996). *Words and Meaning In Yorùbá Religion: Linguistic Connections Between Yorùbá, Ancient Egyptian and Semitic*. Karnak Publishing. London.

______ (1984). *The Sons of the Gods and the Daughters of Men: An Afro-Asiatic Interpretation of Genesis 1-11*. Oribis Books. Maryknoll, MY.

______ (2001). *Yorùbá Names: Their Meaning and their Structure*. Sefer Books LTD. Ibidan, Nigeria.

PYYSALO, Jouna. (2013). *System PIE: The Primary Phoneme Inventory and Sound Law System for Proto-Indo-European*. University of Helsinki. Porthania.

RINGE, Don. (2006). From *Proto-Indo-European to Proto-Germanic: A Linguistic History of English, Vol. I.* Oxford University Press. New York, NY.

RINGE, Don and ESKA, Joseph F. (2013). *Historical Linguistics: Toward a Twenty-First Century Reintegration*. Cambridge University Press. Cambridge.

SHALOMI-HEN, Racheli. (2006). *The Writing of Gods: The Evolution of Divine Classifiers in the Old Kingdom*. Otto Harrasowitz Verlag. Germany.

SCHENKEL, Wolfgang. "Color terms in ancient Egyptian and Coptic," In: Rober E MacLaury, Gailina V. Paramei, Don Dedrick (Hg.), *Anthropology of Color. Interdisciplinary multilevel modeling*, 2007, pp. 211-228.

THOMPSON, Robert F. (1983). *Flash of the Spirit. African & Afro-American Art & Philosophy.* Random House, Inc. New York, NY.

TINDALE, Christopher W. (2007). *Fallacies and Argument Appraisal*. Cambridge University Press. Cambridge.

VAN SERTIMA, Ivan. (1986). *Great African Thinkers, Vol. 1: Cheikh Anta Diop*. Journal of African Civilizations, June 1986 (Vol. 8, No. 1). NJ.

Websites

Dictionnaire ciLuba
http://www.ciyem.ugent.be/ (French)

Kalenjiin Online Dictionary
http://africanlanguages.com/kalenjin/

Meeussen's Proto-Bantu Reconstructions
http://linguistics.berkeley.edu/CBOLD/Docs/Meeussen.html

Proto-SBB (P. Boyeldieu, P. Nougayrol& P. Palayer 2004); La liste de Swadesh pour le proto-SBB (Sara-Bongo-Bagirmi, branche Soudan Central des langues Nilo-Sahariennes)
http://sumale.vjf.cnrs.fr/NC/Public/pdf/swadesh_SBB.pdf

Thesaurus Linguae Aegyptiae
http://aaew.bbaw.de/

Tower of Babel
http://starling.rinet.ru/

Yorùbá Dictionary
http://www.Yorùbádictionary.com/

𓆎𓅓𓏏𓊖

Chapter 2: Kemet As A Toponym

Wudjau Iry-Maat

Considering the two hypotheses on the meaning of the place-name 𓆎𓅓𓏏𓊖 *km.t* ‘Kemet’ as outlined in the introduction to this volume, this essay will focus on the understanding of *toponyms*, their derived *demonyms*, and the consequence that this understanding has on the two fore mentioned hypotheses.

Toponyms

A **toponym** is defined in *United Nations Conference on the Standardization of Geographical Names* (1974: 68) as “the general name for any place or geographical entity.” The study of toponyms is called **toponymy** and one who studies toponymy is called a **toponymist**. The word toponym is derived from the Greek words tópos (τόπος) ‘place’ and ónoma (ὄνομα) ‘name’, thus a **place name**. Toponymy itself is a branch of **onomastics** which is the broader study of names of all kinds. The coinage of toponyms may be a self-assigned name by locals of a place called an **endonym** or a place name used by one group that differs from the name used by the people who live there called an **exonym**. Toponyms can be further divided by type: e.g., **hydronyms** (from Greek: ὕδωρ, hydor, ‘water’ and ὄνομα, onoma, ‘name’) are toponyms referring to bodies of water and **oronyms** (from Greek: ὄρος, óros, ‘mountain, high ground’ and ὄνομα, onoma, ‘name’) are toponyms referring to mountains. Examples are given in Table 1.

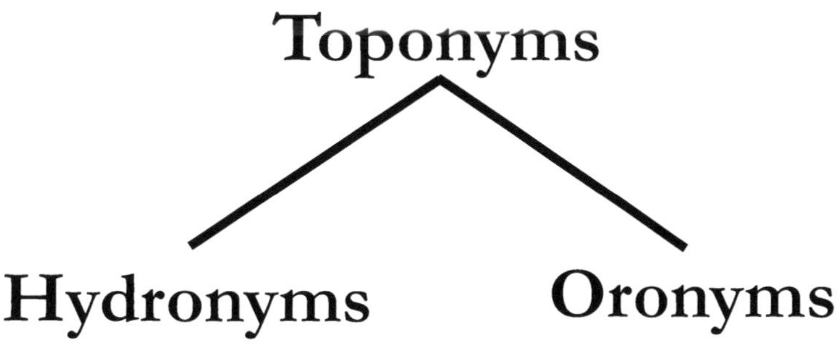

Table 1: Examples of Toponyms

Countries/Continents	Bodies of Water	Mountains
Jamaica	Atlantic Ocean	Mount Everest
Mexico	Pacific Ocean	Mount Fuji
America (U.S.)	Indian Ocean	Mount Kilimanjaro
Canada	Golf of Mexico	Denali
India	Mississippi River	Mont Blanc
Russia	Delaware River	Mount Fitz Roy
Australia	Nile River	Annapurna
Africa	Niger River	Mount Olympus
Europe	Amazon River	Mount Hua
Asia	Mediterranean Sea	Mount Elbrus

It is important to note that in all instances, the **referent**[1] of a toponym is a place and not people. Toponyms are revered for their cartographic, cultural, ethnographic, social, historical, linguistic, economic, political, spiritual, intellectual, scientific and geographical significance. The role of toponyms in modern and classical African societies has been concisely captured by Nna O. Uluocha in the *African Journal of History and Culture Vol. 7 Num 9* p. 180-192 quoted in parts:

> One potent means by which they effectively encoded and communicated cartographic and geographic information was by the use of toponyms (names of places and other geographical features). Thus in vintage African societies place-names were not just chosen arbitrarily; they were carefully chosen to convey specific and useful meanings to the people. This explains why Africans still cherish and attach much significance to local toponyms. Toponyms are an integral component of the cultural identity of a people.
>
> Toponyms fulfill the task of identifying localities thereby distinguishing them from one another... More so, they serve as cartographic labels that can be used for orientation, navigation, recreation, and reference points.
>
> A place-name imparts a certain character on a place. Thus, place-names can also provide a glimpse of the lifestyle led by the people. For instance, geographical names can suggest that a people were "settlers rather than ferocious raiders". In other words, place-names could be used to judge the way of life associated with a people –sedentary or nomadic.
>
> There is a strong link between place-names and environmental/landscape knowledge. Historically, a study of the names of places and topographical features can reveal much about how people viewed and related with the land.
>
> Indigenous African place-names have an enormous treasure of geographical information and knowledge inherent in them. In a typical traditional African society, place-names are used to succinctly describe geographical phenomena. Roden's account of the use of place-names to identify various geographical conditions and features in Uganda typifies what is obtainable in a classic African society. As observed by Roden (1974, 82): "A very prominent group of Ugandan place-names are those which describe or imply the physical characteristics of an area. Relief, climate, soils, hydrology, flora and fauna all feature in names throughout the country. Often the description is in terms of the suitability of an area for human activity–

1 The thing that a word or phrase denotes or stands for.

> the fertility of the soil, the presence of water, reliability of rainfall, suitability for a particular crop, a river or swamp which endangers life, the occurrence of a tree or grass species of value for house building, tool making and handicrafts, and the presence of clay for pottery are all frequent examples. Other names suggest the type of land use, describing a prominent crop, the presence of grazing land and so on."

Today, we are fortunate to have GPS or The Global Positioning System that is a satellite-based radio-navigation system owned by the United States government and operated by the United States Air Force. We have the option of using the GPS in automobiles, smart phones, and other devices to navigate and find our destinations as opposed to using traditional cartographic maps. Prior to our reliance on maps and GPS, it was the role of toponyms to literally communicate vital spatio-temporal information on identity or description of geographical phenomena, location, direction/orientation (both spatial and temporal), relationships, forms and shapes, patterns, magnitude (size), hierarchy, numerical values, proximity, apparent height or depth, temporal dimensions, and so on. These attributes were embedded within the toponym causing it to function as distinguishing markers of location allowing one to know when they have arrived at one location as opposed to another. It is worth reemphasizing that in all instances, the referent of a toponym is a place and not people.

Modern vs. Ancient Egypt

That the country known today as the *Arab Republic of Egypt* was called  *km.t* 'Kemet' in ancient times is not in dispute.[2] In fact, today's Egypt was once known by many names in ancient times. In his seminal work "Kemet and Other Egyptian Terms for Their Land" (1995), Ogden Goelet discusses how the Egyptians' terminology for their country developed over the course of the Old and Middle Kingdoms. We are informed that during the Old Kingdom, "there was an absence of specialized terms distinguishing Egypt from the outside world except for occasional toponyms mostly made from compounds of the word *tꜣ* 'land'" (Goelet 1999: 28). Other terms included 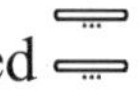 *tꜣ.wy* 'Tawy' [Wb 5, 217.1-219.3], 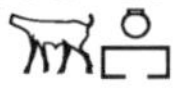 *ẖnw* 'Khenew' [Wb 3, 369.16-370.14], and  *ỉdb.wy* 'Idebwy' [Wb 1, 153.5-6]. It wasn't until the Middle Kingdom somewhere around the period of rulership of King Mentu Hotep of the 11th Dynasty that the term  *km.t* was first used as a place-name for the kingdom (Goelet 1999: 29). In terms of how the place-name was represented in the hieroglyphic and hieratic writing systems we are informed, "The first nonliterary sources mentioning *km.t* seldom employed the , the 'town' sign (sign-list O49) associated with cities and settlements. Most of these early examples of *km.t* either write the word with no determinative or else with the 'cultivated land' sign (sign-list N23)…" (Goelet 1999: 30).

Determinatives

The hieroglyphic writing system did not document vowels in the script. This is similar to Hebrew and Arabic where a person who is familiar with the language can figure out from the context which words are meant by which groups of signs. This is not hard as it seems for example: *yw cn prbbly rd ths sntnc wtht trbl.* The English words *read* and *road* would look alike if written without vowels (rd). We could tell the words apart by adding an extra sign to each that would help us determine which word is meant. For example, a book and street-path with each word respectively. The extra signs added are commonly referred to as **determinatives**. For a more exhaustive explanation of determinatives and the functions of hieroglyphs see *Has the Egyptian Hieroglyphic Writing System Been Deciphered - A Rebuttal* to Walter Williams (2016) by Seshew Maa Ny Medew Netcher. A summary explanation follows:

---

2 As an example of the plethora of citations, in the tale of Sinuhe (B. 26) "I heard the sound of cattle lowing and saw Asiatics, one of their leaders who had been in  *km.t*."

Words spelled with phonographs[3] usually have one or more signs added at the end that serve as classifiers to help **determine** the range of meanings that are applicable to a particular word, hence the name - *determinative*. This helps give the semantic category of the word.

Example of three words with the following three phonographic signs *prt* 'peret':

	prt « Season of Emergence » (disk to show time -)
	prt « fruit, seed » (plough used for sowing -)
	prt « exit » (legs to show motion -)

Example of two words with the following three signs *dpt* 'depet':

	dpt « boat » (determined with boat sign -)
	dpt « taste » (determined with tongue and man with hand to mouth -)

Example of four words with the following two signs *wn* 'wen' « exist »:

	wn « open » (door -)
	wn « hurry » (legs in motion -)
	wn « fault, blame » (sparrow -)
	wn « stripped off » (hair -)

Determinatives are not pronounced, however, as we can see in the examples given, without the added determinative, it would be difficult to know which word is meant. Toponymic determinatives are signs added to words that refer to places or locations making them toponyms. Tables 2 and 3 show examples of toponymic determinatives and Egyptian toponyms respectively.

Table 2: Toponymic Determinatives

Glyph	Code	Description
	N36	canal
	N39	pool
	N31	road
	N21	tongue of land
	N23	irrigation canal
	N25	hills
	O49	town
	N35A	water

3 Phonographs are glyphs that represent not things but the sounds of the language.

Table 3: Egyptian Toponyms[4]

Glyph	Transliteration	Description
	*ḥꜥpy*	Nile River
	*mḥt*	Delta Marshes
	*ḏdwt*	Mendes
	*bꜣst*	Bubastis
	*dp*	Dep
	*ḏdw*	Busiris
	*ỉwnw*	Heliopolis
	*mn-nfr*	Memphis
	*ḫmnw*	Hermopolis
	*ꜣbḏw*	Abydos
	*ꜣbw*	Elephantine
	*ḏsḏstt*	Dakhla Oasis
	*py*	Pe (Buto)
	*bḥd.t*	Behudet
	*msn*	Mesen
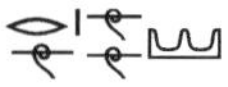	*r-stꜣ.w*	Rosetau
	*ḫm*	Letopolis
	*šd.t*	Crocodilopolis

Ethnonyms

In contrast to toponyms that refer to places or locations, words that refer to groups of people are called **ethnonyms** from the Greek: éthnos (ἔθνος) 'nation' and ónoma (ὄνομα) 'name', thus an ethnic name. Ethnicity is part of human identity. It is human nature for us to be members of groups larger than ourselves. These groups can include our family, neighborhood, profession, tribe, nation, etc. Being a member of a social group gives us a sense of belonging; our sense of who we are is based, at least in part, on those groups of which we are a member. Although there are many alternatives, one useful definition of an ethnic group is:

4 For further examples of Egyptian toponyms, see Budge (2003: 947-1065).

> a firm aggregate of people, historically established on a given territory, possessing in common relatively stable particularities of language and culture, and also recognizing their unity and difference from other similar formations (self-awareness) and expressing this in a self-appointed name (ethnonym). (Dragadze 1990: 207)

Ethnicity is an important aspect of our sense of self, our sense of community and our perceptions of others. Our ethnicity influences how we experience our lives, especially in relation to other people. To unpack the above definition slightly, ethnicity, whether in ancient or modern times, tends to have a number of common characteristics:

- Ethnicity is about contrast: defining who "we" are is only possible by contrasting "us" with some other "them."
- Ethnicity is about perceptions, not necessarily about "facts" or visible, physical features. There are many possible bases for ethnic difference: language, customs, social status, religion, etc.
- Ethnicity is concentric. This means that there are nested layers of belonging to ever larger social groups: you belong to a family which belongs to a community which belongs to a province which belongs to a nation-state, and so on.
- Ethnicity is contextual. This means that the "layer" which is most relevant or applicable to us at any particular time depends on our current context.

Table 4: Examples of Ethnonyms

Kikuyu	Kalenjin	Luo
Maasai	Nuer	Hausa
Han	Ashanti	Igbo
Tswana	Mwenye	Ewe

In the case of the ancient Egyptians, they internally referred to themselves by the ethnonym *rmṯ* 'Remetch' [Wb 2, 421.9-424.14], a name used throughout the kingdom's history. Among the plethora of attestations of its use, *rmṯ* is attested in a text along with vignettes in the popular "Table of Nations" within the fifth division of the *Book of Gates* found in the tombs of King Seti I, King Merneptah, and King Rameses III.

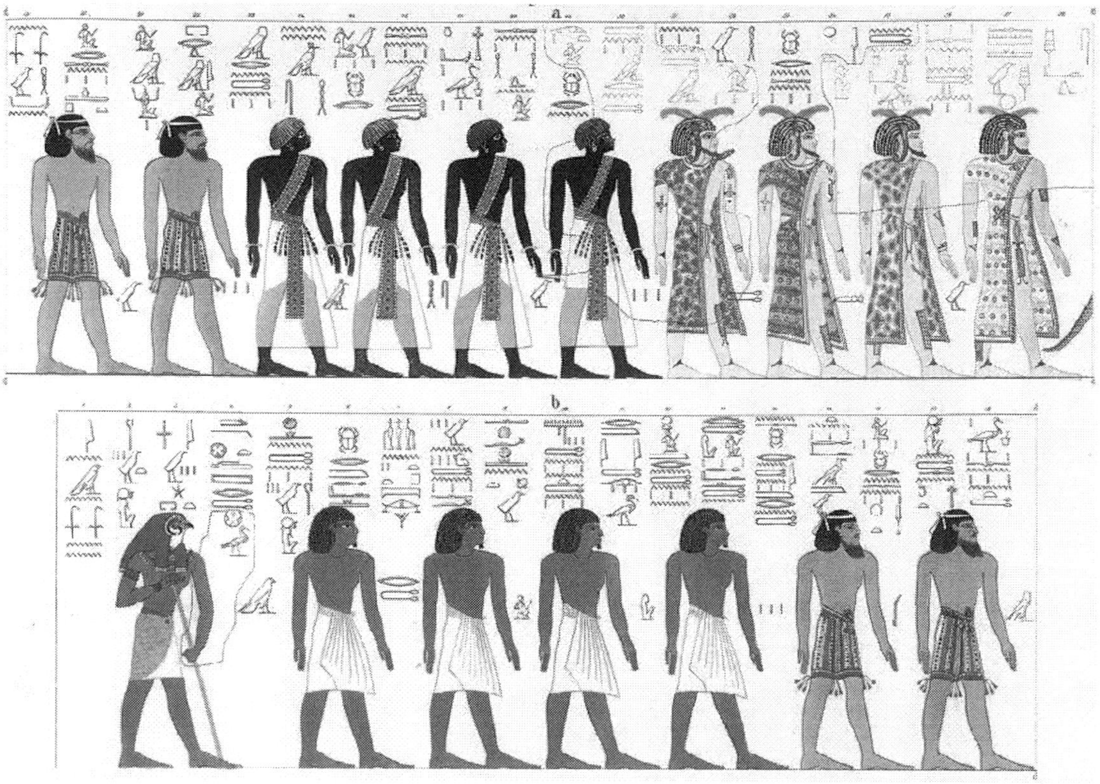

Figure 1: Reproduction of a Partial Scene from the Fifth Division of the Book of Gates in the tomb of Seti I[5]

When the ancient Egyptians distinguished themselves as a cohesive group of people from their close and distant foreign neighbors, they referred to themselves as the *rmṯ* 'Remetch'. In Figure 1, we can see four sets of human groups. On the bottom row, and to the right of the falcon-headed figure, stands four figures with the glyphs + + + in between each person, respectively, facing to the right. Each glyph spells out the ethnonym *rmṯ;* distinguishing the Egyptians from the *ꜣꜥmw*, the *nḥsw*, and the *ṯmḥw*. It is important to note that in all instances, the referent of an ethnonym is a group of people and not a place. For more information on the ethnonym *rmṯ* see essay *The Rōmetch of Kemet: The Agency of Self-Definition: Preliminary Notes* by Sonjedi Ankh-Ra Ary-Nefer.

Demonyms

Words that refer to residents or natives of a particular place and are derived from the name of the place are called **demonyms** from the Greek: dêmos (δῆμος) 'people, tribe' and ónoma (όνομα) 'name'. In other words, demonyms are derived from toponyms and express a relationship between a group of people and their place of origin or residence.

Table 5: Examples of Demonyms

Toponyms		Demonyms
Jamaica	→	Jamaican
Mexico	→	Mexican
America (U.S.)	→	American
Canada	→	Canadian

5 From Giovanni Battista Belzoni: Egyptian race portrayed in the Book of Gates.

India	→	Indian
Russia	→	Russian
Australia	→	Australian
Africa	→	African
Europe	→	European
Asia	→	Asian

As seen in Table 4, the demonyms are formed from the toponyms by adding an additional suffix to denote a relational adjective. In English, it is common to find the suffixes: -(a)n, -ian, -anian, -nian, -in(e), -a(ñ/n)o/a, -e(ñ/n)o/a, -i(ñ/n)o/a, -ite, -(e)r, -ish, etc. added to toponyms to create adjectival forms. We find a similar occurrence in ancient Egyptian where suffixes are added to toponyms to form demonyms or relational adjectives also called **nisbe adjectives**. For a full explanation of relational adjectives and a comprehensive study of Egyptian grammar see Wudjau Iry-Ma'at's forthcoming publication *Ancient Egyptian Orthography & Grammar - A Synchronic Descriptive Grammar of the Older Speech of Kemet* (forthcoming). A summary is sufficient for our understanding within this essay:

Nisbe-adjectives are formed from a substantive (**substantival form**) or preposition (**prepositional form**) by adding the suffix *-y* in the masculine singular which is written before the determinative(s). Like qualifying adjectives, nisbe-adjectives refer to properties and their meaning indicates a relation with the term from which they are derived: "(one) relating to X" or "(that which) relates to X" where X is the term from which they are derived.

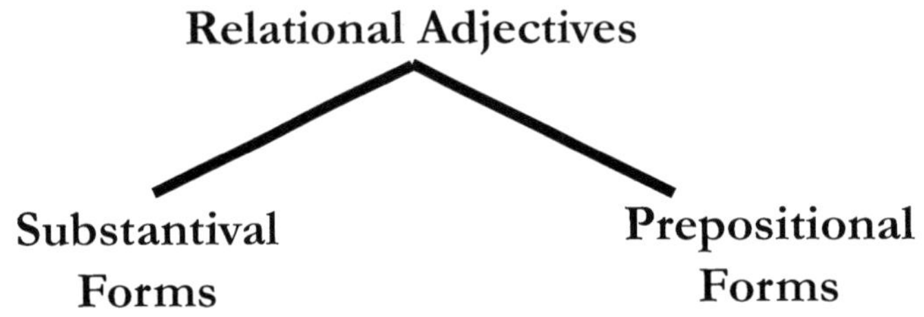

In the case of demonyms the nisbe-adjective is derived from a substantive, which is a toponym and also shows declensional endings for gender and number. The formula is:

substantive(toponym) + y + ending(s)

Since nisbe-adjectives indicate a relation with the term from which they are derived, it is best practice to initially translate them in English according to the following schema:

"(one/ones) relating to X" or "(that/those) which relate to X"
"(one/ones) pertaining to X" or "(that/those) which pertain to X"

...where X is the term from which they are derived, in this case a substantive. In some instances, as with the example of *nἰwty* "(one) relating to the city", this may be reduced to an idiomatic expression such as "a local". Some examples:

Substantive		**Relational Adjective**
ꜣḫ.t « horizon » (f. s.)	→	*ꜣḫty* « (one) pertaining to the horizon » (m. s.)

 *sḫ.t* « field » (f. s.)	→	 *sḫty* « (one) relating to the field, farmer » (m. s.)
 *wpw.t* « message » (f. s.)	→	 *wpwty* « (one) relating to the message, messenger » (m. s.)
 *km.t* « Settlement of Athribis » (f. s.)	→	 *kmty.w* « (those) relating to Kemet, residents of Kemet (Athribis) » (m. pl.)

We draw further attention to the last above example  *km.t*, which is the short form of  *km.t wr.t* or  *km-wr* [Wb 5, 125.12; GDG V, 200 f.; Gomaà, Besiedlung II, 148 ff.] and  the tenth nome of lower Egypt. This area is also known as Athribis from the Greek Ἄθλιβις; Coptic ⲁⲑⲣⲏⲃⲓ, so named from its temple complex  *ḥw.t ḥry-ỉb* [Wb 3, 3.4; GDG IV, 140 f.; Peust, Toponyme, 15]. In the Pyramid Text of Neith PT 674 we read:

ḏswỉ n=k smnty.t ȝs.t ỉs hnỉ n=k hnty nb.t-ḥw.t ỉs

The Mourner will call you as Aset. The Jubiler will cheer you as Nebt-Het.

ꜥḥꜥ=k ḫnty sn.wt mỉn ỉs ꜥḥꜥ=k ḫnty kmty.w ḥpw ỉs

You will stand before the shrines as Min. You will stand before those of Athribis as Apis.

ꜥḥꜥ=k m pḏw š skr-ḥr ỉs

You will stand in the wide lake as Sokar.

In this passage, the demonym  *kmty.w* 'kemetyu' refers to the inhabitants of Athribis (Faulkner 1969: 288, 327; Hanning 1995: 883) not to be mistaken for the entire kingdom of Kemet known after the 11th Dynasty. Later in Edfu at the Ptolemaic temple of Heru there are references to the inhabitants of Kemet by the demonym  *kmty.w.* [WB DZA 30.606.460-480]. See Table 6 for more examples of Egyptian demonyms.

Table 6: Examples of Egyptian Demonyms

Egyptian Toponyms		Egyptian Demonyms
 *dwȝ.t* Duat	→	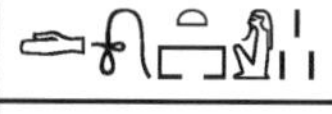 *dwȝty.w* inhabitants of the Duat
 *ỉrm* Irem	→	 *ỉrmty.w* inhabitants of Irem
 *ỉmnt(y).t* The West	→	 *ỉmty.w* inhabitants of the West
 *ȝḫ.t* The Horizon	→	 *ȝḫty.w* inhabitants of the Horizon
 *ỉȝb.t* The East	→	 *ỉȝbty.w* inhabitants of the East
 *wḥȝ.t* Oasis	→	 *wḥȝty.w* inhabitants of the Oasis
 *pwn.t* Punt	→	 *pwnty.w* inhabitants of Punt
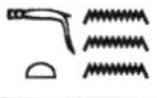 *mḥ.t* The Delta	→	 *mḥty.w* inhabitants of the Delta
 *nỉw.t* The Town	→	 *nỉwty.w* inhabitants of the Town

ḫ3s.t Foreign Land	→	*ḫ3sty.w* inhabitants of Foreign Land

Along with demonyms, there is also **national personification**, an abstraction which is a type of anthropomorphism of a nation. An example of national personification is found in the fourth hymn of the Hymns to Senwoseret (Sesostris) III where the following line appear (Griffith 1898: Plate III, 3-5):

ἰἰ.n=f sꜥnḫ.n=f km.t ḫsr.n=f šnnw=s
He came, he caused the nation of Kemet to live and dispelled its afflictions.

The *=s* pronominal suffix on the word *šnnw* is a 3rd person feminine singular pronoun. It anaphorically[6] refers back to its antecedent[7], which is the word *km.t* and agrees with it in gender and number which is feminine singular. The word *km.t* in this passage is not feminine plural and would not be rendered *km.wt*. In English, specific "it" refers to specific entities that are things or animals, such as "wall," "table," "love," "bear," and so on, as in "he looked at it" (that is, the wall). Abstract "it" does not refer to any entity specifically, as in "he said it because…" Egyptian does not have an equivalent of specific "it." Masculine entities are referred to by masculine pronouns, feminine entities by feminine pronouns. For example, *pr* "house" is masculine and is referred to by the same pronoun as a male human being. In English, however, "house" is referred to by specific "it" and "man" by "he." Whereas specific "it" is either masculine or feminine in Egyptian (depending on the substantive it refers to), abstract (or general, or generic) "it" is expressed by the feminine gender. Accordingly, adjectives referring to abstract "it" assume the -t ending. Examples are as follows:

Table 7: Abstract "It"

	bἰn.t	That which is evil
	ḏw.t	That which is bad
	nfr.t	That which is good

The adjectives in Table 7 refer to a property plus an entity. The properties are "good" and "bad" (*bἰn* and *ḏw* are synonyms). The entity, referred to by -t, is generic "it" in all three instances, *nfr.t* and *bἰn.t* could of course also be translated as "good one" and "bad one," with *-t* referring to an afore-mentioned feminine singular entity. Finally, abstract "it" can also be expressed by prefixing *bw* to certain adjectives. Examples are *bw-nfr* "(that which is) good" and *bw-bἰn* "(that which is) evil." For a more detailed explanation of the abstract "it" and a comprehensive study of Egyptian grammar see Wudjau Iry-Ma'at's forthcoming publication *Ancient Egyptian Orthography & Grammar - A Synchronic Descriptive Grammar of the Older Speech of Kemet* (forthcoming).

Eponyms

Words that refer to a person, place, or thing after whom or after which something is named, or believed to be named are called **eponyms** from the Greek: epi (ἐπί) 'upon, called after' and ónoma (ὄνομα) 'name'. Eponyms do not have referents of their own. A place named after a person is called an **eponymic toponym**

6 An expression whose interpretation depends upon a preceding expression in the context.
7 An expression that gives its meaning to a preform.

(ex: Philippines – Philip II of Spain) and refers to a place and not the person. A body of water that may be named after a person is called an **eponymic hydronym** (ex: Lake Victoria - Queen Victoria). A mountain that may be named after a person is called an **eponymic oronym** (ex: Mt. Everest - Sir George Everest). As seen in these examples, although these places may be named after a person, the referent is a place and never a person or people. A people named after a person is called an **eponymic ethnonym** (ex: Israelites - Israel, the name of Jacob) and refers to a group of people and not the person of whom the group was named.

Table 8: Examples of Eponymous Places

Marshall Islands	John Marshall
Saudi Arabia	Muhammad bin Saud
Austin, Texas	Stephen F. Austin
Berkeley, California	George Berkeley
Pittsburgh, Pennsylvania	William Pitt the Elder
Martin Luther King Jr. Blvd.	Dr. Martin Luther King Jr.
Malcolm X Blvd.	Malcolm X
Kennedy Space Center	John F. Kennedy

Conclusion

Concerning hypothesis 2 (*km.t* referring to "black people"), we understand the name of the ancient kingdom of Egypt as *km.t* is a toponym, which refers to places and locations and not people. This effectively rules out the possibility of the place-name *km.t* referring to "black people". Names referring to groups of people and not places are called ethnonyms be they endonymic or exonymic. When referring to themselves, the ancient Egyptians called themselves by the ethnonym *rmṯ* 'Remetch' "the people". To express their relationship with the kingdom of Kemet or their nationhood the ancient Egyptians used the genitive phrase *rmṯ ny km.t* 'Remetch Ny Kemet' "The people of Kemet" (Sin. B. 33-34) which is also preserved in Sahidic Coptic as ⲣⲙ̄ⲛ̄ⲕⲏⲙⲉ[8]. Demonyms are used to express a relationship with a place or location as in a place of origin or residence. In Egyptian, this is formed using relational adjectives also known as nisbes, which in the case of *km.t* would be rendered in a variation of *kmty.w* or *kmty.w* "the inhabitants of Athribis". Concerning hypothesis 1 (*km.t* referring to "black land"), we come to understand that no scholar made an attempted to prove that the *km* in *km.t* means "black" using sound and established methods in the field of etymology. (see Imhotep 2019).

Selected Bibliography

BUDGE, E.A. Wallis. (2003). *Egyptian Hieroglyphic Dictionary, Vol.1 and II*. Kessinger Publishing, LLC. New York, NY.

DRAGADZE, Tamara (1990). "Some changes in perspectives on ethnicity theory in the 1980's : A brief sketch" In: *Cahiers du monde russe et soviétique*, vol. 31, n°2-3, Avril-Septembre 1990. Regards sur l'anthropologie soviétique. pp. 205-212.

8 See Werner Vycichl, *Dictionnaire Etymologique de la langue copte,* (Belgium : Peeters Publishers), 1983, p. 81

ERMAN, Adolph & Grapow, Hermann. (1971). *Wörterbuch der Aegyptischen Sprache im Auftrage der deutschen Akademien hrsg Bd. I-V*. Unveränderter Nachdruck. Berlin.

FAULKNER, Raymond O. (1969). *The Ancient Egyptian Pyramid Texts*. Clarendon Press, Oxford.

GOELET, Ogden. (1999). "Kemet and Other Egyptian Terms for Their Land." In: R. Chazan, W.W. Hallo, L.H. Schiffman (Eds). *Ki Baruch Hu: Ancient Near Eastern, Biblical, and Judaic Studies in Honor of Baruch A. Levine*. Eisenbrauns. Winona Lake, Indiana. pp. 23-42.

GRIFFITH, Francis L. (1898). *The Petrie Papyri: Hieratic Papyri from Kahun and Gurob (Principally of the Middle Kingdom), vol. 2: Plates*, Quaritch, London.

HANNING, Rainer. (1995). *Grosses Handworterbuch Agyptish-Deutsch : die Sprache der Pharaonen* (2800-950 v. Chr.). Verlag Philipp von Zabern. Mainz.

IMHOTEP, Asar. (2019). *Aaluja, Vol. II: Cyena-Ntu Religion and Philosophy*. Madu-Ndela Press. Philadelphia, PA.

IRY-MAAT, Wudjau (forthcoming). *Ancient Egyptian Orthography & Grammar - A Synchronic Descriptive Grammar of the Older Speech of Kemet.* Heka Multimedia Press, Atlanta GA

Seshew Maa Ny Medew Netcher (2016). *Has The Egyptian Hieroglyphic Writing System Been Deciphered? – A Rebuttal To Walter Williams*. Heka Multimedia Press

ULUOCHA Nna, O. (2015). "Decolonizing place-names: Strategic imperative for preserving indigenous cartography in post-colonial Africa" in African Journal of History and Culture. 7. 180-192.

United Nations (2006). *Manual for the National Standardization of Geographical Names*. United Nations Publications, New York.

Chapter 3: A contribution to the identification of the KM 𓆎 glyph

Asar Imhotep

The objective of this chapter is to identify the inspiration for the I6 𓆎 *km* hieroglyph that is used to write the place-name *Km.t* 𓆎𓅓𓏏𓊖 in ancient Egyptian literature. We will look at a few primary sources and critically examine past arguments that have dominated the discourse concerning the nature of this hieroglyph. We will also offer our own hypothesis and provide the supporting evidence to expand the discussion on the I6 *km* 𓆎 grapheme.

It is F.L. Griffiths, in his text *A Collection of Hieroglyphs: A Contribution to the History of Egyptian Writing* (1898: Plate VI, no. 83; 23f, 31f) that first suggested that the *km* glyph represented a piece of crocodile skin or a fish skin with spines. We must credit Heinrich Schäfer (1897)[1] with the argument that *km* was a depiction of a pile of burning coals and that the adjective "black" derived from it. This became an entry into the famous Erman & Grapow *Wörterbuch der Aegyptischen Sprache Vol. V* (from now on WB): i.e., *km* 𓆎 "pile of burning coals; kiln" [Wb 5, 122.10].[2] Alan Gardiner accepted the crocodile skin hypothesis and this he argued for his I6 designation in his text *Egyptian Grammar: An Introduction to the Study of Hieroglyphs* (1957). Pierre Lacau, *Sur le systeme hieroglyphique* (1954), put a question mark under the entry for *km* with crocodile skin. S. Schott in his *Hieroglyphen*[3], argued that the meaning "black" was associated with a scepter. However, no scholar to my knowledge has been able to verify this claim.[4] Chiekh Anta Diop (1977) accepted Griffiths' proposal, which associated the I6 𓆎 glyph with a pile of burning coals. However, his acceptance was based on the WB entry mentioned above. Most modern ancient Egyptian dictionaries accept the crocodile skin hypothesis, but with reservations. Mubabinge Bilolo (p.c. 2010) believes that the I6 glyph is in fact an animal's paw/foot with claws. This is rendered in ciLuba as *di.kama* "feet with claws; foot tracks/traces, foot of an animal, trace, imprint". It is the hypothesis of the late Alessandra Nibbi (1923-2007) that I find the most compelling concerning the I6 glyph. It is from her hypothesis that we will build on and confirm; although our thesis here modifies hers slightly.

It is in her two articles—"The Hieroglyph Signs GS and KM and their Relationship" (1981)[5] and "A Further Note on the KM Hieroglyph"[6] (1983)—where A. Nibbi argues that the I6 *km* glyph is in fact a stylized hill with vegetation growing from the top. The Old Kingdom (OK) form of the *km* glyph is rendered 𓆏, which is Gardiner sign I6A. Nibbi argues this is a whole mound, which later was represented by a half-mound of black Nile soil (1983: 46).[7] The whole mound looks like the X1 𓏏 glyph, which is believed to be a loaf of

1 As cited in Griffiths (1898).

2 However, there doesn't appear to be any evidence to support this entry. In the WB, this entry refers to a reference known as [Dokument DZA 30.590.310], which is simply a papyrus with a list of hieroglyphic signs.

3 S. Schott *Hieroglyphen: Untersuchungen zum Ursprung der Schrift* (*Abhandlungen der Akademie der Wissenschaften und der Literatur in Minz, Geistes- und Sozialwissenschaliche Klasse*, 1050/Nr. 24 pp. 1707-1862 [I-156]).

4 But note ciLuba: *di.kombo* "travel stick; cane (sign of power); staff, rod, scepter"; ciKam *ḥm* "a club" (weapon; for beating the wash).

5 In: *Gottinger Miszellen, Beiträge zur* ägyptologischen *Diskussion HFT 61 69*. (Göttingen: Universitaet Goettingen), 1981, pp 43-54. From here on out GM.

6 In: *Gottinger Miszellen: Beiträge zur* ägyptologischen *Diskussion HFT 63*. (Göttingen: Universitaet Goettingen), 1983, pp 77-79.

7 She also hypothesized that the Arabic word *kom* "mound" might come from Egyptian *km*. In ancient times, Km.t was known for the large number of mounds it had; so much so that the very country was named after it: *j3.wt* "the mounds (Egypt)" [Wb 1, 26.13]. There was even an area in the Delta called *j3.t* [Gomaà, Besiedlung I,2, 296]. Egypt was still known for

bread. Given its many representations as a base for vegetation, we may need to reconsider the identification of X1 ⌓ as a loaf of bread.

The whole mound glyph was commonly used in the pyramid texts. One can see an example of the whole mound used in the writing of the name of Khasekhem on a base found on an Ashmolean limestone statue.[8] Also along the base of this statue we can see the mound as the base of a plant hieroglyph, which continued on throughout later periods.

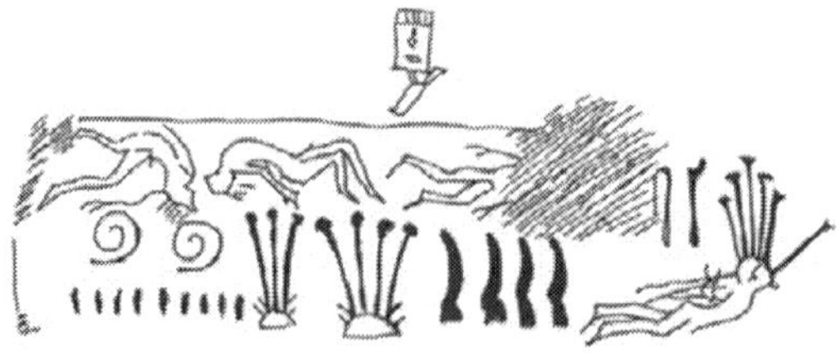

Fig. 1: The inscribed front of the base of the limestone statue of Khasekhem in Oxford, Ashmolean E517.[9]

It appears that the whole mound glyph was used in the early period to represent the base of plant growth as can be seen in the M5 (*tr*), M16A, and M12 (*ḫ3*) hieroglyphs. A whole mound with full vegetation can be seen on a New Kingdom stela of uncertain date. On this stela we have nine crocodiles and nine mounds.

Fig. 2: Limestone stele of the Ramesside period. (aus: Fazzini, "Some Egyptian Reliefs in Brooklyn," in: *Miscellanea Wilbouriana I*, Brooklyn 1972, Fig. 23)

its mounds as late as the 1800s. As D.G. Hogarth ["Three Northern Delta Nomes," In: *Journal of Hellenic Studies*, 24, (1904), 1-19] and A. Edwards [*Pharaohs, Fellahs, and Explorers* (1891), p. 6] both emphasized that the Delta contained hundreds of mounds. The word *Km.t*, at least evidenced by the OK form, may be related to these mounds. Cf. ciLuba *mu.kùnà*, which means "mountain; hill," but also "bank, shore; Lingala *ngomba* "hill" > *li.ngomba* "society"; Basaa *komba* "region, country";

8 Quibell, Hierakonopolis I, Plates XXXIX and XL.

9 After B. Adams, in: *JEA* 76, 1990, 161-163.

That the mound is often depicted with various representations of plant life can be seen in the following example from Sir Alan Gardiner's *Egyptian Grammar: Being An Introduction to the Study of Hieroglyphs* (1957: 489). Here Gardiner shows a variation of the mound glyph (N29) and states the following:

> "mound[10] of earth with shrubs[11]" Ideogram or determinative in , variant *j3t* "mound."

Here the shrubs look more like blocks attached to the mound. But in other representations, the shrubs or vegetation is represented by vertical or curved strokes. They represent rhizomes of a budding plant.

A rhizome is a continuously growing horizontal underground stem which puts out lateral shoots and adventitious roots at intervals. It is a modified subterranean plant stem that sends out roots and shoots from its nodes. These rhizomes were often represented by simple vertical strokes, which can be seen in the M31 (Dyn. XVIII) and M32 (Dyn. XII) "stylized rhizome of lotus, *rd*" hieroglyphs (Fitcher, 1999: 35; Gardiner 1957: 483). These glyphs have the consonant values of *rd* and derives from the words *rd* "to grow" [Wb 2, 462.20-463.7; FCD 154; Lesko, Dictionary II, 73] and *rd* "plants" [Wb 2, 463.8-10]. It is these rhizomes that we see present on the I6 and I6A *km* glyphs that have been stylized.

The more common variations of the *km* glyph can be seen in the following table with their Gardiner sign numbers. These representations range from the OK to the Ptolemaic period.

Table 1: Variations of the I6 glyph

I6A		I6C	
I6		I6D	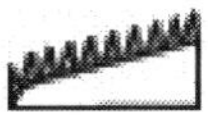
I6B		I120	
		I137	

While the I6A form dominated the Old Kingdom, and periodically resurfaced throughout pharaonic history, the dominate form in usage came during the Middle Kingdom (MK) under the standard I6 form. It is this form that is commonly mistaken for a crocodile's tail (see the tails in Fig. 2 above and compare them with I6B in Table 1). What Nibbi (1981, 1983) suggests is that the MK form is an adaptation of the Aa15 *gs* hieroglyph, which she calls a half-mound.

Table 2: *gs* variants

Aa13		Aa15	
Aa16		Aa1	

These variants are found in Gardiner's "unclassified" section of his sign-list. Kurt Sethe suggested that the hieroglyph depicted two ribs of an oryx. But this hypothesis was later rejected by Gardiner. Nibbi suggests that this glyph represents one side of a river bank: thus, giving us the meaning of "side; half." Throughout the MK and NK representations, the two forms *gs* and *km* began to differentiate more. A major difference

10 *Exx.* Dyn. IV, *Medum* ii; Dyn. XVIII, *D.* el *B.* 116. Note the mounds were such an important landscape that this root became a name for the country of Egypt: e.g., *j3.wt* "the mounds" (Egypt) [Wb 1, 26.13]

11 *Bull.* 3, 145.

between the two glyphs (besides the presence or absence of the vegetation) is that the *gs* glyph is opened on one side, while the *km* glyph is closed. We argue here that the open side of *gs* and the closed side of *km* are the areas where the land is. Where the glyph curves is the land's edge and where the river begins.

As further noted by Nibbi:

> To emphasize the great similarity between the gs and km signs during the Middle Kingdom, both in hieroglyphic and hieratic writing, we must note that the hieratic version of the standard shape for gs (as in our fig. 1 e) is read as km in the Papyrus Reisner I. This is clearly to be seen in Plate 18, lines 4 and 6, and in Plate 17 throughout. The sign is read as gs only in the lists (Section H) and Plate 15, line 16 (Section I). It is listed also in the writing of these signs during the Middle Kingdom in hieroglyphic and hieratic versions. (Nibbi, 1981: 44)

Therefore, *gs* was also known as *km,* although it was rarely called it in the Egyptian literature. The close similarity of the MK *km* variants to *gs* can be seen in the following representations (after Nibbi 1981).

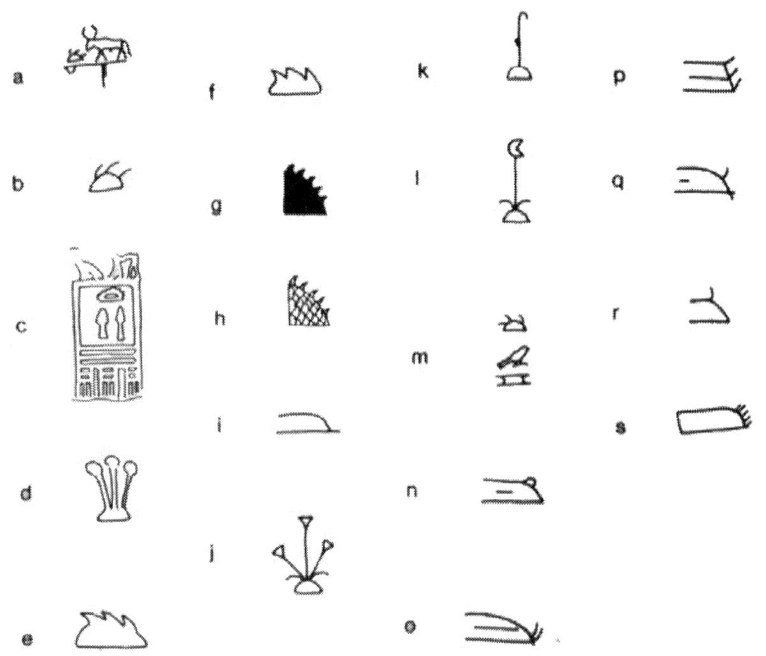

Fig. 3: representations of the *km* mound/river bank glyphs.[12]

For Nibbi, the *gs* and MK *km* glyphs represent, still, a mound. It is here where I differ with Nibbi. I argue that the *gs* and *km* glyphs from the MK are stylized representations of a river bank, but from the *aspective* view looking down from above. The part of the glyph that is perceived as a hill slope from the *perspective* view, is in fact the curvature of the river's edge when looked at from an areal view.

12 References from Nibbi (1981: 52): **a)** Sethe, Pyramidentexte I, 556c; **b)** ibid. 1998b; **c)** Ayrton, Currelly and Weigall, Abydos III, Plate IX, no. 9; **d)** Petrie, Royal Tombs I, Plate XXIII; **e)** Gardiner, Peet and Cerny, Inscriptions of the Sinai I, Plate XXV a; **f)** Maspero, Mem. Mission Arch. Francaise au Caire I, Plate XIII, line 3; g) Newberry, Beni Hasan III, Plate VI, no. 102; **h)** ibid. no. 103; **i)** Kelly Simpson, Papyrus Reisner I, Plate 17; **j)** Wörterbuch 3, 8ff; **k)** Gardiner, Grammar, Signlist M5; **l)** ibid. M12; **m)** Naville, Deir El Bahari V, Plate 128; **n)** Cerny and Gardiner, Hieratic Ostraca, Plate IX A; **o)** ibid. Plate XVII A, 4; **p)** ibid. Plate XXXIX A, 1 recto; **q)** ibid. Plate LXX, 2; **r)** Ll. Griffiths, Two Hieratic Papyri, I The Sign Papyrus, Plate IV, P XIX, line 3; **s)** Wörterbuch 5, 122ff.

Fig. 4: The Nile River

The projecting strokes found at the edge of the *km* I6 hieroglyph are the shrubs found at the edge of the river along the side of the bank. This explains why on the MK versions of the I6 glyph the shrubs are on the curved edge. Whereas, on the OK forms the plant shrubs can be found on one side or across the entire mound. It is clear that the OK I6A glyph is an entirely different glyph than the I6 hieroglyph. The changing and updating of glyphs was a common practice throughout ancient Egyptian history.[13] Thus, the focus in the OK was the plants on a mound (Arabic *ʔakam-at* "hill" (assimilation of vowels **ʔakam- < *ʔikam-*); Boghom (Chadic) *kya(a)m* "mountain"; Tigrinya (Ethiopic) *kuma* "mountain"; Lingala *ngomba* "mountain; hill") and in the MK the focus was on the plants along the river's edge.[14]

Evidence for this interpretation can be seen in an even later rendition of the *km* hieroglyph, Gardiner code I6C and I6D. A detailed representation of this glyph in a more expansive scene can be viewed from a Medinet Habu relief of Rameses III hunting wild bulls (Fig. 5 below).[15]

---

13 For example, we learn that the OK classifiers N20 (*jdb, wḏb*), N21 (*jdb, wḏb*), and N22 (*jdb, sḫt, wḏb*) are what became the N36 glyph in Dyn. VIII and N23 in Dyn. XI (the time when *km.t* first appears as a name designation for the country) (Gardiner, 1957: 488). As artistic motival designs, hieroglyphs undergo stylistic changes which is evident in modifications to its represented forms. Provided that art is a living entity, and reflects social predilections, over the course of three millennia we would expect to see a variety of stylistic changes in artistic motifs over the course of the culture.

14 Cf. ciLuba *mu.kùnà* "mountain, hill" and "bank, shore."

15 This is the exterior, first pylon, south tower, west facing. See James H Breasted, (Ed.). *Medinet Habu, Vol. II: Later Historical Records of Ramses III.* (Chicago: The University of Chicago Press). 1932, Plates 117 and 130.

Fig. 5: Rameses III hunting wild bulls.

What we see in this scene is a number of hunters chasing after wild bulls. The bulls are being chased to the edge of the Nile River, which is clearly indicated by the variety of fish on the right-hand side. Along the edge of the shore we see the very same plant spikes that we see in the I6D hieroglyph, which again is a variation of the I6 hieroglyph from the middle kingdom (just in more detail). What's also telling about this scene is that it is clearly in the delta area of Egypt. We know by two key features: 1) the presence of wild bulls, and 2) the type of plants being depicted in the image.

It is known that the Delta region of Km.t is primarily where the cattle roamed and grazed and where the herdsmen dwelled. The Nile Valley is not really able to support large amounts of wild cattle as it is primarily desert, except along the edge of the Nile River. Toby Wilkinson, in his text *Early Dynastic Egypt* (2001: 124), informs us of the cattle association in Lower Km.t:

> The Delta seems to have been closely associated with cattle rearing – as reflected in the prevalence of cattle amongst the emblems of the Delta nomes – and *ḥwt iḥw* may have been the most important cattle-producing centre of early times. A further connection between the western Delta and cattle rearing may be indicated by the herds depicted on the so-called 'Libyan palette' (Wenke and Brewer, 1996: 268). Another estate connected with cattle, 'the estate of the golden cattle of the dual king' (*ḥwt iḥw-nbw nswt-bity Mr-*(*p-*)*biꜣ*) is mentioned on sealings of Anedjib from Abydos (Petrie 1900: pl. XXVIII.73.4).

F.D.P. Wicker, in his text *Egypt and the Mountain of the Moon* (1990), also verifies this association.

> The Egyptians who settled in lower Egypt must have been herdsmen first and agriculturists second, whereas the opposite seems to have been the case in upper Egypt. It can be seen that their red crown derived from a calf skin of their red, long-horned cattle, cattle still to be found in Ankole and Toro in Uganda, and in neighbouring territories. (F.D.P. Wicker, 1990: 39)

That the Delta was home to cattle and the herdsmen was well known, even to the ancient Greeks. Heliodorus of Emesa wrote a romance or novel called Æthiopica that takes place in Aethiopia. However, much of the story takes place in Egypt. Book 2 of the novel is titled "The flight from the marsh" (i.e., Lower Km.t; the

Delta) and in it he tells us that the delta area was inhabited mainly by herdsmen and brigands on every tip of land emerging from the water. An example can be seen in Book 2 starting at line 71:

> 'You shall hear it,' said he; 'I only wish that thrifty Nausicles were here too, whom I have often by divers delays deluded, being very desirous to hear this tale.' When Cnemon heard Nausicles named, he asked where he was then. 'He is gone a hunting,' quoth the old man. 'What manner of hunting?' said he. 'Of wild beasts,' replied the other, 'very cruel, which he called indeed men and herdsmen, who live by theft and can hardly be trapped, for that they use the marsh as their den and cave.' 'Whereof doth he accuse them?' said he. 'Of the taking away of a leman of his,' he answered, 'whom he brought from Athens, one called Thisbe.'[16]

As we can see here, not only is the presence of 'wild beasts' (i.e., cattle, bulls, etc.) a feature of the Delta marshes, so is the activity of hunting these animals, as can be seen in the Rameses III bull hunting scene (Fig. 5) above.

Growing out of the ground where the buds are depicted along the shore of Fig. 5, we see the M17 𓇋 reed plants in full-bloom. The common reed, *Phragmites australis* (synonym *P. communis*), is a tall perennial grass and grows abundantly in the marshy and salty areas of Egypt.[17] This tall grass grows about four meters in height and spreads by long rhizomes to form extensive reed swamps. These roots bind the soil alongside streams, which prevents erosion, and gradually builds up to the level of the bank providing flood control. It has bamboo-like canes and it was very useful for light constructions, arrow shafts, and pens. What is characteristic about this plant is how its light brown plume-like inflorescences *bend* in the wind and the grassy leaves rustle (Hepper, 2009: 35). This is important to note because this is what is being depicted when we see the plant stems bending on the I6A glyph.

As noted by Barakat & Aziz (2010: 204), these reeds arise from just a few seeds or small plantings. They are generally found clustered at the *water's edge*, providing a haven for water birds. This would explain why the MK variations of the *km* glyph have the plant buds on the edges of the glyph sprouting upward as we see in Fig. 6.

Fig. 6: A rendering of the word Km.t from the bottom of a pilon at the temple of Luxor.
Image by the author.

Another thing to note is that reeds may also be used as *food*. The young roots are eaten raw or cooked like potatoes. They are often dried and *ground* for porridge. The leaves can be used as an herb or dried and *powdered* and added to cereal flour (*ibid.*). This explains the following lexical items in ciKam via paronymy:

16 http://www.elfinspell.com/HeliodorusBk2.html. From The Æthiopica: "Heliodorus - An Aethiopian Romance" translated by Thomas Underdowne (Anno 1587), revised and partly rewritten by F. A. Wright; George Routledge & Sons Ltd.: London; New York: E. P. Dutton & Co.; [with additional corrections in the online edition by S. Rhoads;] pp. 47-86.

17 F. Nigel Hepper, *Pharaoh's Flowers: The Botanical Treasures of Tutankamun, 2nd Edition*, (: KWS Publishers). 2009, p. 35.; Mala Barakat and Ibrahim Abdel Aziz, *Guide to Plants of Ancient Egypt*, (Alexandrina: CULTNAT-Center for Documentation of Cultural and Natural Heritage). 2010, p. 204.

km.*y*	"food"
km.*t*	"grain or plant"
km.*w*	"seeds or fruit of *km* plant"
s.***kmkm***	"destruction; annihilation" (***gm****gm* "to smash; to break; to tear" > *w****gm*** "powder; crushed grain)

Thus, the I6 *km* glyph points us to a variety of concepts, which includes food, plants, and the shore line. As noted previously, the spikes coming out of the I6 glyph are simply plant bud or stems (rhizomes) and on many other hieroglyphs these plants are depicted as vertical lines. The rhizomes or first plant buds are present in the M20  *sḫ.t* glyph. This is essentially the *km* glyph from a different angle (perspective view) and with the added reed leaves. This is not surprising given that *sḫ.t* and *km.t* are dialectical variations of the same word from a common ancestor. Given the principle of transitivity, *sḫ.t* is also a variant pronunciation of N22 *jdb/wḏb*, which is also a variant of *km.t: i.e., wḏb* "shore; river bank"[18]; *db.w* "bank" [Wb 5, 434.8; AEO I, 9*].[19] We can demonstrate this fact by first establishing the sound correspondences. As is discussed in Imhotep (2019), the form *j.db* derives from *w.ḏb* where *ḏ* > *d* and *j* ~ *w* interchange. Hence, we observe the following sound-meaning correspondences:

Table 3:

ciKam ***ḏ-b***	**ciKam** ***k-m***	**Correspondences**
ḏb.*ꜣ* "to replace; to reimburse; to repay" ***ḏb***.*w* "income" ***ḏb***.*ꜣ.w* "compensation; payments"	***km*** "to pay"	ḏ- : k- -b : -m
ḏb.*ꜣ* "to be blocked; to block"	*j*.***km*** "shield; protection" (instrument prefix *j*-)	ḏ- : k- -b : -m
ḏb.*ꜣ* "food offerings"	***km***.*y* "food"	ḏ- : k- -b : -m
ḏb.*ꜣ.w* "leaves; foliage" ***ḏb***.*ꜥ* "a plant for incense"	***km***.*t* "grain or plant"	ḏ- : k- -b : -m
ḏb.*ꜥ.w* "blame; reproach"	***km*** "complain"	ḏ- : k- -b : -m
ḏb *ḏb* "to crush" (by treading)	*s*.***kmkm*** "destruction" ~ ***gm****gm* "to crush"	ḏ- : k- -b : -m

We thus confirm that the consonant sequence *k-m* internally corresponds to *ḏ-b*, which would also correspond to *d-b* given *ḏ* > *d*. The following table confirms this hypothesis:

Table 4:

km.*y*(*t*)		food
db.*ḥ*		foodstuff

18 We note that *j*- and *w*- interchange in ciKam.

19 The word *dbb* "to stop up" [Wb 5, 436.3; vgl. FCD 311; Dévaud, Étymologie, 17 f.] might be a reflex.

skmkm	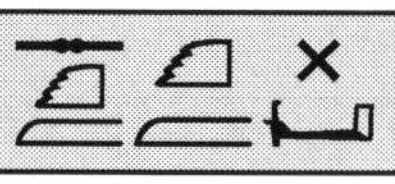	destruction, annihilation
*h̲.**db***		kill, execute
****km***		hair
***db**.nt*	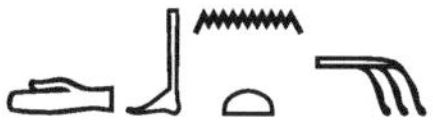	lock of hair, sidelock (of child)
***km**.w*		seeds or fruit of *km* plant
***db**.yt*		foliage, plant, flower
***km**.t*		A woman's disease; gynaecological disorder
*ḥ.**db**.wt*		illness, retention (of urine)?

Given the *k-m* and *d-b* correspondences, we would predict that there will be some *d-b* forms that pertain to land, banks, or shores. This is exactly what we find in the Egyptian lexicon as Table 5 confirms below.

Table 5:

***Km**.t*	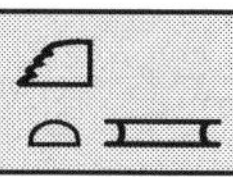	
***db**.wy*		bank, shoreline
*j.**db**.wy*		the two riverbanks, the two shores
*j.**db***		riverbank, riparian land, shore (of flood)
***Km**.t*	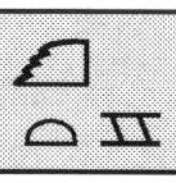	
*ḳ.**db***		rented arable land
*ḳ.**db**.yt*		arable land lease
*ḥ.**db***		highlands
*j.**db***		field, meadow, bank
*n.**db**.wt*		area, foundations, precincts, extent
*h̲.**db**.y*		Farmer, Stockman (i.e., a worker of the land)

These are very important correspondences because it highlights the fact that there are a number of internal cognates to the word Km.t in the ancient Egyptian lexicon (doublets; borrowings?). We thus can compare ***Km**.t* with ***ndb**.wt* "area, extent" [Wb 2, 368.7-10; FCD 143; Wilson, Ptol. Lexikon, 561 f.], and ***ndb*** "area, territory, piece of land, foundation" [Wb 2, 368.2-4; Wilson, Ptol. Lexicon, 561-2]. This is confirmed by the fact that all terms use the same classifier. Thus, we cannot interpret Km.t as anything other than a type of "land" because it belongs to the land class.

Given that Egyptologists like to focus on the black alluvial soil when referring to Km.t, we note the following terms: *db.yt* "sand, mud"; *db.n(w)* "dung, clay, mud." We note, however, that there is no *km* "mud, clay, sand" in the modern Egyptian dictionaries. But given our analysis in Imhotep (2019), with Km.t being defined as "damp ground, irrigable land; a new pasturage with abundance of grass and water," *db.yt* "mud" would be an obvious reflex, well within our semantic range. This form is also a dialectical variant of *ʿmʿ.t* "mud; muddy ground; a kind of arable soil" [Wb 1, 185.17; FCD 42; Harris, Minerals, 200 f.; AEO I, *10 f.; KoptHWb 144]; *jm* "mud; clay" [Wb 1, 78.2-3; Harris, Minerals, 200] as *d* and ʿ interchange in ciKam.[20] It should be noted that neither *db.yt* or *ʿmʿ.t* "mud, muddy ground; clay"[21] employs the D3 hair glyph to reference blackness, or color in general. This is further confirmation that *km.t* doesn't refer to the "blackness" of the soil, but rather its "wetness."

Table 6: ʿ- – *k*- correspondences in the C1 position.[22]

ciKam ʿ-*m*	ciKam *k-m*	ciLuba	Correspondences
ʿm.w "a very juicy fruit (?) (med.)"; *ʿm.ȝ* "a plant (a very juicy fruit?) (med.)"	*km.w* "seeds or fruit of *km* plant";	-	ʿ - : k- : ?- -m : -m : -?
ʿm.w "a food"	*km.yw* "food"	-	ʿ - : k- : ?- -m : -m : -?
ʿm.ȝ "beer jug"[1]	*km.t* "a jar"	*ci.ngulu* "great pot; jar" *	ʿ - : k- : g- -m : -m : -l
ʿmʿm "a container (for bread)"	‖	*nnyungù* "pot; jug" **	ʿ - : k- : ɲ- -m : -m : -ŋ
ʿmȝ "turn sour, spoil, go bad"	*s.kmkm* "destruction" ~ *gmgm* "crush, smash, to tear"	*-nyanga* "damage, destroy, deteriorate, spoil, defile; mess up; abuse, maltreat";	ʿ- : k- : ɲ- -m : -m : -ŋ
ʿwȝ "to rot; to spoil" [Wb 1, 172.3-5]	‖	*nyanguka* "spoiling, being spoiled, damaged"; "be destroyed, abused, mistreated"	ʿ- : k- : ɲ- -w : -m : -ŋ
ʿmʿ.t "virgin"	-	*-jimà* "virgin"	ʿ- : ?- : j- -m : -? : -m
ʿm "something that makes a noise"	-	*mu.kuma* "report; noise; sound of a gun"	ʿ- : ?- : k- -m : -? : -m
ʿmʿʿ "kernel (of grain); (date) pip (med.)"	*km.t* "grain or plant"	*di.tungù* "seed" (of corn, of millet"	ʿ- : ?- : t- -m : -? : -ŋ

20 For an in-depth analysis, see Helmut Satzinger "Egyptian 'Ayin in Variation with D," in: *LingAeg* 6 (1999), pp. 141-151. See also Mboli (2010) for an expansive commentary.

21 Cf. M-E *ʿmʿ.t* "mud, muddy ground; clay" with Yoruba *amọ* "clay, mud," Urhobo *oma* "clayey soil," ciLuba *di.kama* "damp ground," Arabic *hama'* "mud."

22 All the relevant sound correspondences for ciLuba and ciKam are complete in Imhotep (2019).

ʿmʿ "a kind of beer"	[Cf. *nḏm* "a kind of beer"]	*mu.sèlè(à)* "beer; malt, corn seed sprouted to make beer"	ʿ- : ?- : s- -m : -? : -l
ʿmj "to smear; to seal"	-	*-kànga* "close; seal";	ʿ- : ?- : k- -m : -? : -ŋ
		jiba "close; seal"	ʿ- : ?- : j- -m : -? : -b
ʿmʿm "to rub (feet)"	*gmgm* "to finger, to caress"	*-kula* "rub; grind; massage"	ʿ- : g- : k- -m : -m : -l

*23 | **24

We want to continue our demonstration that *sẖ.t* and *km.t* are dialectical variants. We have already established that *b* and *m* correspond in ciKam in the C_2 position. This will become vitally important further on in our discourse. For now, we note that the [*ḏ*] sound in ciKam derived from [g] (Loprieno 1995: 31, Anselin 2001, Bernal 2006: 194). Thus, we can expect *k-m* ~ *g-m* correspondences, which are established below.[25]

Table 7: *km* ~ *gm* correspondences

Dialect *k-m*	Dialect *g-m/w*	Correspondences
***km**.t* "complete eye"	***gm**.ḥ* "eye"; "to catch sight of"	k- : g- -m : -m
	***gm**.j* "to find; to discover"	
	***ggw**.j* "marvel; stare"	
*s.**kmkm*** "destruction; annihilation"	***gmgm*** "to smash; to break; to tear"	k- : g- -m : -m
km "duty; profit"	***gm*** "invoice; sum; account"	k- : g- -m : -m
***km**.y(t)* "food"	***gm*** "produce; product"	k- : g- -m : -m
	***gw**.ꜣ* "a bread"	
***km**.w* "a mineral"	***gm**.ḥ* "specially shaped stone as part of a doorway"	k- : g- -m : -m
***km**.w* "a substance" (med.)		
***km**.yt* "herd of cattle"	***gw*** "bull"	k- : g- -m : -w
***km**.t* "a jar"	***gn**.t* "a vessel"	k- : g- -m : -n

Given the above data, it is safe to say that *km.t* and *gbb* "earth, field" are also cognates (keeping in mind *b* ~ *m*). In addition, the fact that many dialects of ciKam formed prior to the dynastic period, alongside the fact that these dialects have been interacting for a long time with neighboring languages (related and unrelated), we find doublets of these terms throughout ciKam. By knowing the dialectical variants of the forms of *km.t*, we can better answer important questions regarding its meaning and usage: including the very hieroglyph itself. We have to now establish that Egyptian *k-* in *km.t* and *s-* in *sẖ.t* correspond in the C_1 position. From there, we will establish that *-ẖ* and *-m* correspond in the C_2 position.

23 Cf. Sumerian *gir* "a large jar."

24 Cf. ciLuba *lu.samba* "cooking pot; pot"; Sumerian *sab* "an oil jar."

25 Note that *k* ~ *g* interchange in Demotic. But note that many of these *g-m* forms are from the OK and MK.

Table 8: ciKam *k* ~ *s* correspondences in C_1

km "profit; to pay"	*j.**sw*** "payment"	k- : s- -m : -w
km "complain"	***sm**.j* "to report; to complain; reporter"	k- : s- -m : -m
km.t "Egypt"	***sm**.j* "pasture"	k- : s- -m : -m
***km**.yw* "herd of cattle"	***sm**.ꜣ* "wild bull" ***sm**.ꜣ.t* "wild cow"	k- : s- -m : -m
***km**.t* "*black* cattle (divine herd)"		
***kf**.j* "to open; to unlock"; "to gape (of a wound)"	***zf*** "to cut open; to slaughter"	k- : z- -f : -f
km.t "a woman's disease"	***sw**.t* "symptom of an affliction"	k- : s- -m : -w
km "crocodile tail"?	***sw**.y* "crocodile"	k- : s- -m : -w
*s.**kmkm*** "destruction, annihilation"	***sm**.ꜥ* "thrust; knock; push; shove" ***sm**.ꜣ* "to slay"	k- : s- -m : -m
***km**.t* "grain or plant" (Budge, 788a) ***km**.w* "seeds or fruit of *km* plant"	***sm**.w* "plants; vegetables; pasture" ***sm**.yt* "herb(s); herbage"	k- : s- -m : -m
*s.**km*** "to grow old; be wise"	***smsm*** "the oldest"	k- : s- -m : -m

Given that *k-m* corresponds to *s-m*, it is no coincidence that *sm* is also the consonant value of the M21 glyph and is the root of *sm.w* "pastures, plants, herbage, vegetables, herb." The only real difference between *sm* and *sḫ.t* is the presence of the rhizomes in the *sḫ.t* glyph. That Egyptian *k-* corresponds with *s-* can be seen also via ciLuba-Bantu, as we see below.

Table 9: ciKam *k-m* and ciLuba *s-l* correspondences

ciKam	ciLuba	Correspondences
km.t "dorsal fin"	*mu.sàlàlà* "fin; flipper";	k- : s- -m : -l
km "service; duty; work,"	*-sala* "to do; to work; to serve" (Lower Kongo); *ku-sadila* (*kosalela* in Lingala)	k- : s- -m : -l
km "to pay,"	*-sela* "to pay the dowry for a wife"	k- : s- -m : -l
km.t "Egypt" ?	*mu.sulu* "river, brook, stream, creek"	k- : s- -m : -l
km "complete; put an end to"	*-sùla* "to be finished, completed"	k- : s- -m : -l

	ku.sala "at the end of, the point of, limit of, at the boundary of, at the border/edge/margin/bank/ beach or shore/coast" (*ku-* loc. Prefix)	
*s.**km*** "to bring to an end; to finish out; spend"	*-sùdi.**sha*** "go through, until the end, finish"	k- : s- -m : -l [l+i>di]

Given these correspondences, we should see the same in reverse: i.e., ciKam *s-* corresponding to ciLuba *k-* in the C_1 position.

Table 10: ciKam *s-* and ciLuba *k-* C_1 correspondences

ciKam	ciLuba	Correspondences
st.w "arrow; dart"	*mu-**keta*** "arrow"	s- : k- -t : -t
stj.t "shrine; temple"	*lu.**kita*** "tomb; shrine"	s- : k- -t : -t
st.w "shooting"	*-**kòka*** "to shoot"	s- : k- -t : -k
	*-**kùma*** "to shoot" (a gun)	
sṯ.j "to drag; to pull; to usher in"	*-**kòka*** "to drag"	s- : k- -t : -k
zr "ram"; *zr.t* "sheep; ewe"	*mu-**kooku*** "sheep"	s- : k- -t : -k
zḥ.t "heard of sheep"		
st.j "leg" (esp. of Osiris)	*mu.**kalu*** "leg"	s- : k- -t : -l
st.j "light up; illuminate"	*-aa**kisha*** "light up" (< *-aaka* "catch fire") [*-sha* caus. suff.]	s- : k- -t : -ø
st.ꜣ "flame; lamp"; "to heat; to set afire"		

As noted in Imhotep (2019), *-ẖ* in ciKam internally corresponds to virtually all the labials in the C_2 position: i.e., *-m*, *-b*, *-w*, *-f*, and *-p*. We can see a few examples below.

ꜣẖ "beer, wine"	*j.**nb*** "drink"
	*s.**nw*** "wine of Pelusium"
	*s.**rf*** "beer"
***ꜣẖ**.t* "uraeus serpent"	***nb**.d* "to coil, to wind around"[26]
***ꜣẖ**.t* "field; meadow"	*j.**nb**.w* "a field"
	*ḥ.**nb*** "farmland"
***ꜣẖ**.t* "brilliant eye of God"	*w.**nb*** "a part of the eye"
***ꜣẖ**.y* "plants"	***nb**.w* "a plant" (med.)
***ꜣẖ**.t* "urn"[27]; "a libation vessel"	***nb**.t* "a vessel"
***ꜣẖ**.j* "sweep up"	***nw**.y* "to collect"
***ꜣẖ**.w* "sunlight, sunshine"	***nw**.t* "sunrays; light rays"
***ꜣẖ**.t* "flame, fire"	*s.**nb*** "to burn"

26 Words for snake in ciKam derive from words meaning to "go" or "to coil." See Imhotep (2019).
27 (containing the pieces of Osiris).

	***nb**.j* "to be aflame"
***3ẖ**.t* "provisions" (bread)	*ḏ.**nb*** "pastry"
	*s.**nw*** "bread offerings"
	*s.**rf**.t* "warm bread"
3ẖ3ẖ "flourish/blossom, become green"	*w.**nb*** "flower; blossom"[28]

We have mentioned the interchange between *m* ~ *b* in ciKam. Given the *ẖ* ~ *b* correspondence, we can also predict *ẖ* ~ *b* ~ *m*. We note the following:

nẖnẖ	"fling/hurl; massacre/butcher"[29]	*n-ẖ*
nm.t	"place of slaughter"[30]	*n-m*
nm.tjw	"executioner"[31]	*n-m*
npḏ	"to slaughter"	*n-p*
ȝẖ.t	"flame; fire"	*ȝ-ẖ*
ȝb.w	"brand; branding iron" (brazier deter.)	*ȝ-b*
ȝm.w	"(scorching) heat; flame"	*ȝ-m*
ʿẖ.j	"to fly"	*ʿ-ẖ*
ʿẖ.j	"fly away"	*ʿ-ẖ*
ʿp.j	"fly" (verb).	*ʿ-p*
jb	"to wish; to suppose"	*j-b*
ȝb.w	"wish(es); vow"[32]	*ȝ-b*
ẖr.t	"wish"	*ẖ-r*
mr.j	"to wish; to love"	*m-r*[33]

Thus, we have firmly established, by the presence of regular sound-meaning correspondences, that the *k-m* sequence would correspond to *s-ẖ* given the data above. We now confirm our prediction.

Table 11: *km* ~ *sẖ* comparisons

km.yt "herd of cattle"	*sẖ.tjw* "a kind of cattle"	k- : s- -m : -ẖ
km.t "cow"	*sẖ.tjt* "cow goddess"	k- : s- -m : -ẖ
km "perform, work"	*sẖ.tj* "peasant; fieldworker; fowler"	k- : s- -m : -ẖ
km.y(t) "food"	*sẖ.t* "(offering) bread"	k- : s- -m : -ẖ
km.t , "Egypt"	*sẖ.t* "marshland; country"	k- : s- -m : -ẖ
Km.t	*sẖ.t* "field"	k- : s- -m : -ẖ

28 These correspondences reveal that the dialectical variant of *rẖ.yt* "common folk; humankind; subjects (of the king)" [Wb 2, 447.9-448.2; AEO I, 98* ff.] is *rmṯ* "human being; man" [Wb 2, 421.9-424.14], *rmṯ.t* "humankind, people" [Wb 2, 424.17-18; ONB 291] as /ẖ/ corresponds with labials: e.g., /m/, /b/, and the nasal /n/.

29 [Wb 2, 312.12-13; Lesko, Dictionary II, 29; KoptHWb 368, Anm.5].

30 [Wb 2, 264.1-9; FCD 132; Van der Molen, Dictionary of Coffin Texts, 226; Wilson, Ptol. Lexikon, 521 f.].

31 Wb 2, 264.10; LGG IV, 237].

32 *ȝb.t* "wish(es); vow"; *ȝb.j* "to wish for; to covet."

33 *ẖr* and *mr* are simply the inverse of *ȝb*.

[ciLuba: *-kùma* "spinning, making thread; make fabrics, weave"]	*sẖ.t* "weave, mould (bricks), lay out (foundations)"	

Given the cognancy of *km.t* with *sẖ.t*, the M20 *sẖ.t* glyph thus provides valuable insight into the I6 *km* hieroglyph. With the evidence from the Rameses III temple at Medinet Habu, we can safely argue that *sẖ.t* is simply a *perspective* view of *km.t*, which is an *aspective* view of the same reality. Note as well that *sẖ.t*, like *km.t*, is never written with any color classifiers to reference any 'black soil'. If *km.t* meant "black land," then so would its dialectical variants *jdb.wy, db.yt, sẖ.t*, etc. We can apply this method to a different set of lexemes, which will further demonstrate our point.

In Imhotep (2019), I demonstrate that M-E /k/ corresponds with M-E /ḥ/ and /ẖ/. I show that the consonant sequence *k-m* corresponds to both *ḥ-m* and *m-ḥ* consonant sequences. Given the principle of transitivity, and our establishment of *k-m* to *s-m* above, we can predict that we will find a series of *s-m* correspondences with both *ḥ-m* and *m-ḥ* consonant sequences in ciKam. The following table confirms our hypothesis.

Table 12:

s-m	*m-ḥ ~ ḥ-m*	Correspondences
sm "priest"	*mḥ.j* "a priest"	s- : -ḥ -m : m-
sm "high priest of Ptah at Memphis"		
sm.wj "a priest"		
sm "attention, care, help"; "to help; to succour"	*mḥ.j* "to care for; to be concerned about"	s- : -ḥ -m : m-
sm "pay attention, respect, value"	*mẖ* "honor, respect" (someone)	s- : -ẖ -m : m-
sm.t "respect; esteem"		
sm.y "respected"	*ḥm* "Majesty"	s- : ḥ- -m : -m
sm "image; likeness"	*ẖm* "sacred image"	s- : -ẖ -m : m-
sm.yt "herb(s), herbage"	*mh.w.t* "a fruit"	s- : -ḥ -m : m-
	mh.j.t "a fruit"	
sm.w "plants; vegetables; pasture"	*ḥmꜣ.w* "a plant" (fenugreek?)	s- : ḥ- -m : -m
	ḥm.w "a plant" (fenugreek?)	
sm.ꜣ "God's barque"	*mḥ* "a ship"	s- : -ḥ -m : m-
	mḥ "the bark of Sokar"	
	mḥ "a boat"	
zm.ꜣ "to copulate with"	*ḥm.s* "phallus" (*-s* suffix of body parts)	z- : -ḥ -m : m-
ms "child"	*mḥ* "child"	m- : m- s- : ḥ-

sm "joy, pleasure"; "be happy"	*n.ḥm* "joy; pleasure; rejoicing"	s- : -ḥ -m : m-
zm.ꜣ "wildlife"	*ḥm.t* "an animal"	s- : ḥ- -m : -m
sm.ꜣ "wild bull"	*ḥm.z* "crocodile"	
zm.ꜣ.t "wild cow"	*ḥm.t* "cow"	z- : ḥ- -m : -m
zm.ꜣ "rod, pole, staff"	*ḥm.t* "stake"	s- : ḥ- -m : -m
	ḥm.t.j "spear"	
sm.ꜣ "to slay"	*ḥm.n* "butcher"	s- : ḥ- -m : -m
	ḥm.z "to slay; to mutilate"	
sm.j "pasture"	*mḥ* "plot of land; field"	s- : -ḥ -m : m-
sm.j "to report; to complain"; "acknowledgment; accusation"; "reporter"	*w.ḥm* repeat, report (of speech), do again	s- : ḥ- -m : -m
sm.ꜣ "scalp; temple (of the head)	*gm.ꜣ* "temple of the head; temporal bone" (remember *km* ~ *gm*)	z- : g- -m : -m
sm.j "to swallow"	*ẖm.w* "swallow, eat, devour"	z- : ẖ- -m : -m

We have thus systematically eliminated chance from our correspondence set. It is on this ground that we can argue, also, that a dialectical variant of *Km.t* is in fact *mḥ.t* "arable field" [Edfou VIII, 9.15]; *mḥ.t* "marshes of the delta" [Wb 2, 125.4-5]; *mḥ.w* "parcel of land, land plot," *mḥ.ty* "north." The association of *mḥ.t* with "arable fields" and the "delta marshes" correlates visually with the I6 *km* glyph as discussed throughout this essay. We thus strongly argue that the I6 glyph depicts one side of the Nile River, probably at the edge of the Delta marshes. We note also that the projectiles are rhizomes or plant buds in association with the marsh reeds or vegetation in general. Given the bull hunting scene of Rameses III (Fig. 5), we find it no coincidence, either, the presence of the word *mḥ.w* "hunter; sportsman" ~ *mḥ.y* "holy bull" (< *km.y* "(black) bull"). Note that all of these dialectical forms, just like the variations of *Km.t*, do not employ a single color classifier.

On the O49 "city" hieroglyph

In my 2014 essay "A Lesson in Egyptian Determinatives: The Case of KMT," I argued that the O49 *njw.t* symbol was in fact a stylized intersection of canals and *not* a town crossroads as is commonly argued in the Egyptological literature. This was important to note because of its interchangeability with both the N23 *tꜣ* "irrigated land" and N36 *mr* "canal" classifiers, as can be seen in the following example.

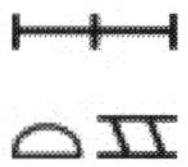	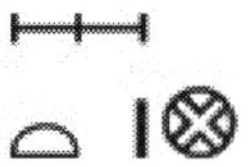
sp3.t "district, nome, necropolis"	*sp3.t* "district, nome"[2]

I also argued that the O49 *njw.t* symbol was, in essence, a stylized contraction of the N24 *sp3.t*[34] glyph. The variations on this glyph help to conceptualize its connection.

Table 13: Irrigated land classifiers

	N24C	
	N24D	
	N24G	
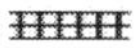	N24	*ḥsp, sp3t, t3-wr*

The *sp3.t* classifier can be seen in one of the renderings for *Km-wr* and many of the other nomes of ancient Km.t. The interchangeability of these graphemes underscores an interconnection between the symbols that the ancient Egyptians exploited at every juncture. Given that Km.t is written with the N23, N36, and O49 classifiers, it clarifies for us that the concept of Km.t has to deal with a type of land with the presence of an abundance of water: enough to develop an irrigation system to sustain life and agriculture.

Since my 2014 publication, I came across a journal article by Jonathan Van Lepp that independently supports the arguments I made in 2014. The title of the article is, "Is the Hieroglyphic Sign *niwt* a Village with Cross-Roads?"[35] In this text, Van Lepp supports the notion that the Egyptian O49 *njw.t* symbol is, in fact, a series of interconnected water channels.[36] But what he adds to the discourse is the notion that it represents, in total, a water basin (1997: 93).

34 N24 is also rendered *ḥsp* as in *ḥzp* "garden (plot); meadow" [Wb 3, 162.4-8; Wilson, Ptol. Lexikon, 678]. Again, we see the interchangeability with the form *ḥsp* "garden," where the N24 sign is replaced with N23 "irrigated land."

35 In: *Gottinger Miszellen: Beitrage zur Agyptologischen Diskussion*, Heft 158, (Göttingen), 1997, pp. 91-100.

36 He is not alone in this reinterpretation of the sign, see also K. Kuhlmann, 'Die Stadt als Sinnbild der Nachbarschaft', *MDAIK* 47, 1991, pp. 217-226 where the sign is cited as a circular dam protecting an urban conglomerate.

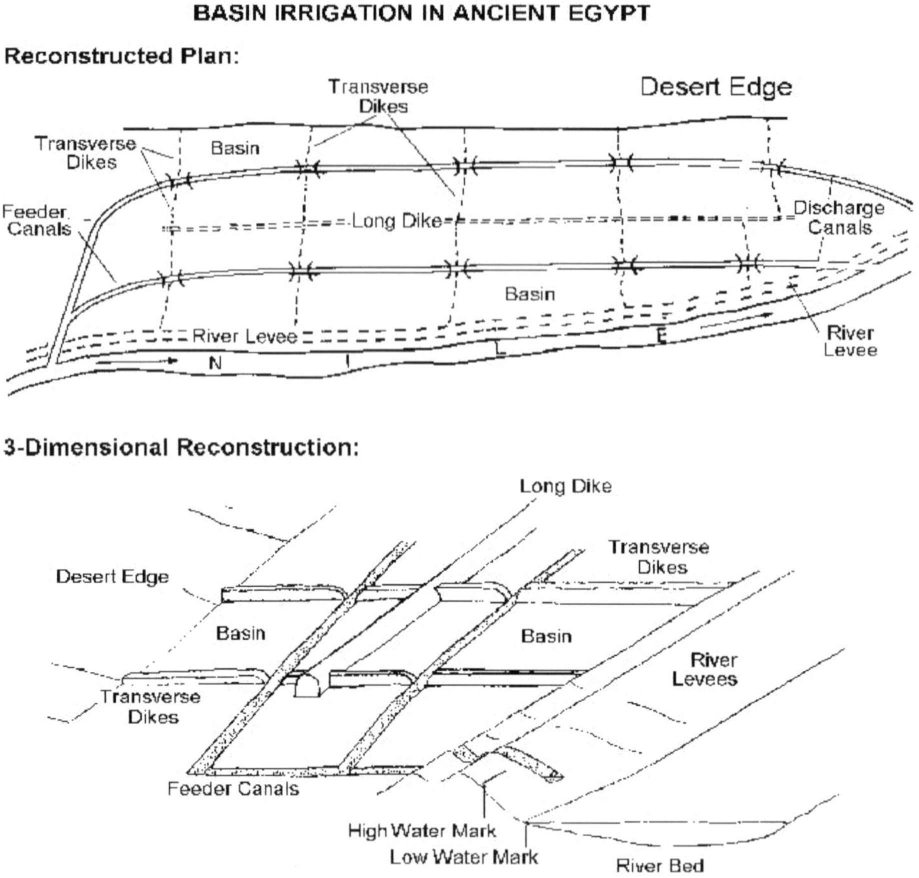

Fig. 7: Basin irrigation plan in ancient Egypt.

The Egyptians practiced a form of water management called basin irrigation, which is a productive adaptation of the natural rise and fall of the river. They constructed a network of earthen banks that formed basins of various sizes. Some of these earthen banks were parallel to the river and some perpendicular to it. The flow of the flood water was regulated by sluices that would direct the water into a basin. Here the water would sit for a month or so until the soil was saturated. The water would then be drained off to a near-by canal and the farmers would plant their crops on the now drained plot of land.

Van Lepp argues that the O49 ⊗ *njw.t* symbol is a 'modern' representation of water motifs on pottery whose design evolved since the predynastic period. As early as the Amratian period (4000-3500 BCE), circle motifs were often associated with water as we can see in Fig.# below (Van Lepp, 1997: 93-94).

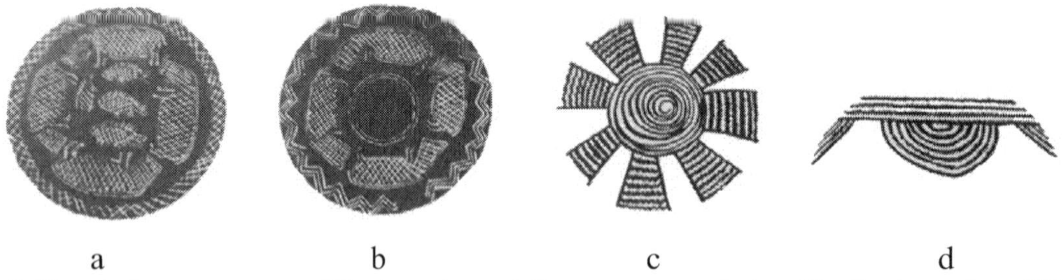

Fig. 8: The circle as a water motif in Amratian and Gerzean pottery design. Fig. 8a drawn from W.M.F. Petrie, *Prehistoric Egypt* (London, 1920), pl. XVIII, 71; fig. 8b drawn from Petrie, *Ibid.*, pl. XVIII, 72; fig. 8c drawn from A. Lythgoe, *The Predynastic Cemetery N 7000 Naga-ed-Der*, pl. IV (Berkeley and Los Angeles, 1965); fig. 8d drawn from Lythogoe, *Ibid.*, 150e.

Both figures 8a and 8b portray hippopotami in their aquatic environment with a circular water motif as the outer border. In 8a we see the hippopotami surrounding fish in the center. In 8b the fish are replaced with two circular lines, which must represent water. Fig. 8c displays water emanating in six courses from a circle enclosing a spiral. Fig. 8d is found in Gerzean art (3400-3100 BCE) where half circles composed of the water motif are attached to longitudinal water, which Van Lepp assumes is the Nile (1997, 93).

Although the circle motif, as a representation of water, continued throughout the predynastic period, we are introduced to a cross motif in early Amratian times inside the circle as seen in Fig.# below.

Fig. 9: Circle with water motif and cross pattern (Van Lepp, 1997: 94).

We can see from this image a primitive representation of what became the *njw.t* hieroglyph. Baumgartel interpreted the circle to be a pond filled with water.[37] However, she did not attempt to analyze the cross motif. Van Lepp concludes that these cross patterns are canals used to distribute water from collection in basins to fields for irrigation.[38] Essentially, the *njw.t* hieroglyph is a circle with two *mr* signs crossed at right angles.

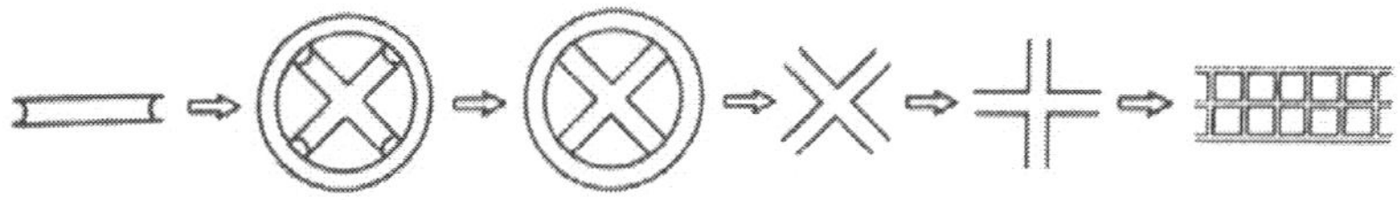

Fig. 10: Formation of *njw.t* and *sp3.t* signs using existing glyphs. Drawing after Van Lepp (1997: 97).

The *mr* sign is simply a single row in a series of earthen banks. In the early period the *mr* sign was represented with a series of vertical walls, which divided the sign into sections. The number of walls varied: usually from 4 to 6. In a sealing from the reign of Ka'a we find the *mr* hieroglyph divided into five sections. This is the same number later found in the *sp3.t* hieroglyph.

Fig. 11: *mr* sign from inscription of Ka'a, drawn from Petrie, *RT I*. pl. XXIX, 84.

Lastly, there are a few instances where the O49 glyph was depicted in color. From the color variations of this motif, it is clear that water and land are the focus of this hieroglyph and not a "cross-road" from a city plan. In the OK tomb of Ptahotep, the *njw.t* sign is painted in black lines with a blue interior cross pattern. In the tomb of Akhethotep, which is nearby, the color black is substituted by the color red. Van Lepp interprets these colors to represent the black and red soils found throughout Egypt. The presence of additional triangles on the four corners of the motif are land formations. These are common in OK versions of the *njw.t* symbol. Evidence to support this notion may be found on an earlier Amratian pottery design that has strong correlations with the later *njw.t* symbol.[39] In a later New Kingdom tomb of Nefertari, there is a rendition of the *njw.t* sign with slight modifications to the traditional patterns. Firstly, the triangles in the four corners are no longer present and the coloration has changed. The interior cross-pattern is green and the outside lines are now blue. It is clear that

37 E. Baumgartel, *The Cultures of Predynastic Egypt I* (London, 1947) I, 65ff.

38 Van Lepp, "Evidence for artificial Irrigation in Amratian Art," *JARCE 32* (1995), 198ff.

39 See Van Lepp (1997: 95, Fig. 6); W.M.F. Petrie, *Prehistoric Egypt*, pl. XV, 59.

the interior coloration was meant to signify irrigated land, which was provided water from the surrounding canals. Figure 11 below highlights these features mentioned. Given this publication is in black and white, the appropriate features are labeled for the reader.

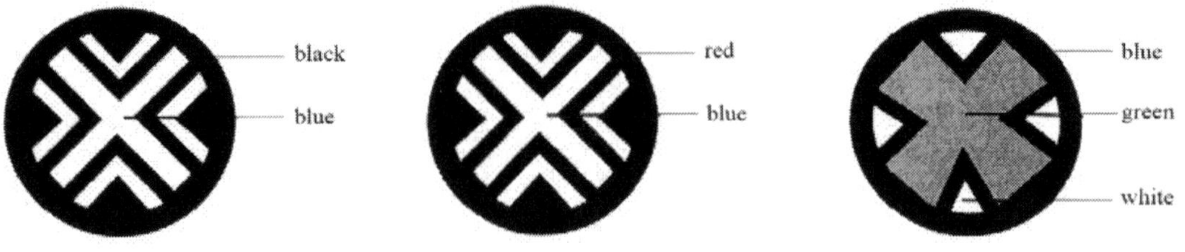

Ptahhotep Akhethotep Nefertari

Fig. 12: *Njw.t* sign as painted in the tombs of Ptahhotep, Akhethotep, and Nefertari; Ptahhotep drawn from Davies, *The Mastaba of Ptahhotep and Akhethotep at Saqqarah I* (London, 1900), pl. XVIII, 404; Akhethotep drawn from description in Davies, *ibid.*, 27; Nefertari drawn from K. Michalowski, *Art of Ancient Egypt* (New York, 1968), pl. 26.

The evidence is overwhelming that the O49 glyph has to deal with the intersection of water canals (*mr.w*) of a water basin. This is important because, as stated earlier, the N23, N36, and O49 classifiers are in fact stylistic variations of the same concept: i.e., irrigated land. 99% of all renderings of the place-name Km.t are classed by one of these three glyphs, which indicates that Km.t has to deal with a *place* with a particular geographical feature (i.e., the presence of water for crops) and not *people* as proposed by Diop (1977). It also indicates that the focus was not on the soil of the land or its color. If the focus was on soil, we would see the presence of the N33A classifier as in the word *jtn* "soil, dirt, dust" (Wb 1, 145, see MedWb 109, KoptHWb, 53). The primary focus is the presence of water as all three classifiers highlight the path of water. This explains why the place-name Km.t is never terminated with any of the known color classifiers: i.e., the N33 ° "grain of sand; pellet," or D3 "(black) hair" hieroglyphs. Given that the word Km.t "Egypt" is the name of a place, it can never be used to describe anything: it only references a location.

The presence of the form [Wb 5, 127.20], with the seated man and woman classifiers, from the Kahun papyrus,[40] then, must convey another idea. In the literary *Hymns to Sesotris III* (Dyn. XII), we find the following passage (pl. III, 3-5):[41]

> *jj.n.f n.n ḥkꜣ.n.f* *Km.t rdj.n.f dšr.t m ꜥb.f jj.n.f n.n mkj.n.f tꜣwy sgrḥ.n.f jdbwy jj.n.f n.n sꜥnḫ.n.f* *Km.t ḫsr.n.f šnww.s*
>
> "It was (after) he had ruled Egypt, and (after) he had put the Desert in his company, that he came to us. It was (after) he had protected the Two Lands, and (after) he had pacified the Two Banks, that he came to us. It was (after) he had caused Egypt to live and (after) he had removed its needs, that he came to us."

The way this passage is worded lets us know that it is talking about the *state* as a political entity, and not the nisbe-adjective form *Km.tjw* "those of Kemet." This is supported by the fact that *km.t* is used in the same manner as all of the other political locations in the text. The names *dšr.t, tꜣ.wy* and *jdb.wy* in the original text do not employ personal determinatives. Furthermore, after the second sentence containing the word *Km.t*, it refers back to the word *Km.t* by means of a third-person singular feminine suffix pronoun *.s* "its." If it spoke about the people, we would expect *.sn* "their, they, them," not "its."

40 London, Petrie Museum of Egyptian Archaeology pUC London 32157.

41 F.L. Griffith, *The Petrie Papyri: Hieratic Papyri from Kahun and Gruob* (Principally of the Middle Kingdom), vol. 2: Plates (London: Quaritch, 1898) pl. 3: a facsimile appears in G. Moller, *Hieratische Lesetucke fur den akademischen Gebrauch*, vol. 1: *Altund MittelhieratischeTexte* (2d. ed.; Leipzing: Hinrichs, 1927) pl. 5; conveniently transcribed in K. Sethe, *Agyptische Lesestucke zum Gebrauch im akademischen Unterricht* (Leipzing: Hinrichs, 1928) 37.

In the online *Thesaurus Linguae Aegyptiae's*[42] assessment of the Kahun papyrus, the translators rendered the *.s* suffix pronoun as (seine) "his, its." The critical line examined is provided as such from the website:

> [III, 5] *<<jy.n>> =<<f>> sꜥnḫ.n =f km,t ḫsr.n =f šn,w =s*
> (Er ist gekommen), nachdem er (die Bewohner) Ägyptens belebt und **ihre** (wörtl.: seine (sc. Ägyptens)) Not beseitigt hat.
>
> [(He has come) after he has animated (the inhabitants) of Egypt and has eliminated **their** (literally: its (eg. The Egyptians) needs.]

There is some additional commentary in a note for the above line. The translators state the following:

> *Km.t* ist wieder mit Personendeterminativ und determinierenden Pluralstrichen geschrieben, so dass wieder die Landesbewohner, nicht das Land als solches gemeint ist (vgl. den Kommentar zu Zeile III, 4). Das Suffixpronomen hinter *šnw* verdeutlicht aber, dass grammatikalisch das singularische Wort *Km.t*: "Ägypten" vorliegt.
>
> [*Km.t* is again written with a personal determinative and plural strokes, so that again the country dwellers, not the country as such are meant (see the comment to line III, 4). However, the suffix pronoun behind *šnw* makes it clear that **grammatically** the singular word *Km.t*: "Egypt" exists.]

While they acknowledge that the grammar forces them to render the reference to Km.t as a singular collective entity, they instead translate the third-person singular feminine suffix *.s* as "their" solely on the presence of the seated man and woman in Km.t . It is for this reason, also, that they stuck in the phrase (die Bewohner) "the inhabitants of" Egypt, although this is not present in the text. In other words, the translators are reading into the text instead of reading from it.

It should be noted that the presence of the plural strokes does not always indicate the plural, but the abstract or collective.[43] This can be seen in a few ancient Egyptian lexemes.

 *jꜣi* "to adore"

 *jꜣi.w* "adoration"

 *jni* "to bring"

 *jn.(n)w* "production, tribute"[3]

It is even present in words for land or field: e.g., *jnb* 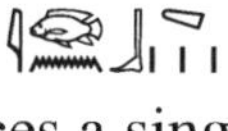 "field." The presence of the plural strokes in *jnb* does not indicate multiple fields. The word references a single field. Thus, the presence of the plural strokes only indicates the abstractness of the concept of a field: the place. The same feature is present in the word *mḥ.t*  "field" [Edfou VIII, 9.15]. We've already established that the word *mḥ.t* is a dialectical variant of the word *km.t*. As we can see here, the presence of the plural strokes does not render the word plural. We see this even with words with the seated man and woman classifiers.

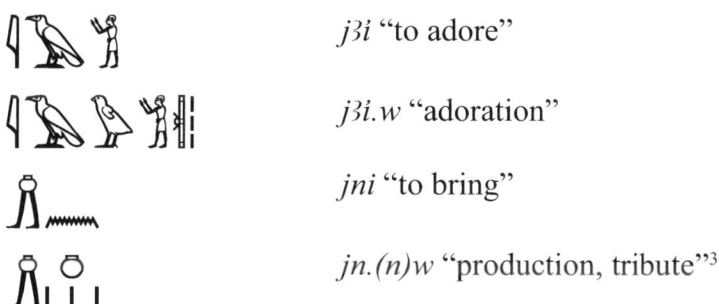

---

42 Visit: http://aaew.bbaw.de/tla/servlet/GetCtxt?u=imhotep06&f=0&l=0&tc=369&db=0&ws=435&mv=4.

43 "A collective noun is a noun that refers to a group of entities that may be considered either as individuals or as one larger entity." For example, CLUB: "it is a large club"; "They are a large club." See the SIL glossary of terms: https://glossary.sil.org/term/collective-noun (retrieved 4/7/2019).

ḏ.t "serf"

nḏ.t "subject; slave; serf"

rmṯ-jz.t "workman"

rmṯ-nb "anyone, someone; somebody"

rmṯ-mšꜥ "conscript, military rank, Schulman"

The presence of the plural strokes as a classifier is often accompanied by a *-w* or a *-t* suffix to the root. In other words, the presence of this classifier coincides with a grammatical morpheme: i.e., *-w* and *-t*. Both *-w* and *-t* can be used for the abstract and the collective. The abstract and collective also derives from a morpheme for "place" (< land < foot). Thus, when we see the presence of the seated man and woman above the plural strokes in Km.t, it is still a singular idea as is evident in *ḏ.t* "serf"; *nḏ.t* "subject; slave; serf," for example. We argue here that Km.t is to be understood as the *nation* in the abstract and not the inhabitants of. Grammatically, if we wanted to say "the inhabitants of Km.t" we would have to write *Km.tjw*. However, although this form is present in the literature, the word *Km.tjw* is never used to refer to the Egyptians as a whole.[44] They referred to themselves simply as *rmṯ*.

There are many Egyptological publications that render *Km.tjw* as "Egyptians," including the Erman & Grapow *Wörterbuch*. However, scholars have come to realize that this is a mistranslation and only refers to a nome called *Km.t* (short for *Km.t-Wr.t*) in Lower Egypt. In many publications it is simply known as *Km-wr* [Wb 5, 125.12; GDG V, 200 f.; Gomaà, Besiedlung II, 148 ff.]. The capital of this nome was known as *ḥw.t-ḥr.j-jb.t*, which became Greek *Athribis*.[45] Essentially the entire area became known as Athribis and is today called Tell Atrib. Rainer Hanning, in his *Die Sprache der Pharaonen, Großes Handwörterbuch Ägyptisch-Deutsch* (2800-950 v. Chr.), correctly defines *km.tjw* as "Leute aus Athribis" (People from Athribis) (1995: 883). Jean Leclant, in his journal article "À La Pyramide de Pépi I, La Paroi Nord du Passage A-F (Antichambre —Chambre Funéraire),"[46] confirms as well that *Km.tjw* is in fact a reference to Athribis based on his analysis of the pyramid text of Pepi I. He informs us that:

> s) On a longtemps interprete *Kmtiw* par << Egyptiens >>. Un essai d'interpretation par Otto du § 1998 (=N 797 a ete presente dans *Beitrage zur Geschichte der Stierkulte in Agypten,* p. 14-5. Faulker, *Ancient Egyptian Pyramid Texts*, p. 288 et 327, a suppose qu'il s'agissait de << the people of Athribis >>. La presence du taureau en palimpseste dans notre nouveau texte de Pepi I confirmerait cette hypothese. Km-wr est mentionne en tant que tel dans *Pyr.* § 556 c.
>
> [We have (for a) long time interpreted *Kmtiw* as "Egyptians." An interpretation in an essay by Otto § 1998 (= N 797) was presented in *Beiträge zur Geschichte der Stierkulte* in *Ägypten*, p. 14-5. Faulkner, *Ancient Egyptian Pyramid Texts*, p. 288 and 327, assumed that it was "the people of Athribis." The presence of the bull in palimpsest in our new text of Pepi I confirms this hypothesis. *Km-wr* is mentioned as such in *Pyr.* § 556c.] (Leclant, 1975: 146)

Chiekh Anta Diop, as noted in the proceedings of the 1974 Cairo Symposium,[47] attempted to argue that *Km.tjw* meant "the Blacks" or "Egyptians" based on the WB entry of Erman & Grapow (1957) (UNESCO, 1978: 78).

44 However, there may be one exception to this rule as evidenced in the Ptolemaic period (see Chapter 2 this volume).

45 For an in-depth discussion on the nome of Athribis, see Pascal Vernus, *Athribis: Textes et Documents Relatifs à la Geographie, aux Cultes, et à L'Histoire D'Une Ville du Delta Egyptien à L'Epoque Pharaonique*, (France: Institut Francais D'Archeologie Orientale Du Caire), 1978.

46 In: *Ruvue D'Egyptologie*, Tome 27, 1975, pp. 137-149.

47 See UNESCO, *The Peopling of Ancient Egypt and the Deciphering of Meroitic Script*, (Paris, UNESCO), 1978.

It was Surge Sauneron, the great Egyptologist and grammarian, who had to inform Diop of the grammatical rule pertaining to the nisbe adjectival form of the word *Km.tjw*. As noted by the conference reporter:

> Professor Sauneron, intervening in the course of a lively exchange of views on linguistic matters between Professors Abdalla and Diop stated that in Egyptian KM (feminine KMT) meant 'black'; the masculine plural was KMU (Kemou), and the feminine plural KMNT. The form KMTYW could mean only two things: 'those of Kmt,' 'the inhabitants of Kmt ('the black country'). It was a derived adjective (nisba) formed from a geographical term which had become a proper name; it was not necessarily 'felt' with its original meaning. To designate 'black people', the Egyptians would have said Kmt or Kmu, not Kmtyw. In any case, they never used this adjective to indicate the black people of the African hinterland whom they knew about from the time of the New Kingdom onwards; nor, in general, did they use names of colours to distinguish different peoples. (UNESCO, 1978: 82-83)

As is currently understood by the extant literature, the nisbe form of *km.tjw* can only refer to those who belong to or are associated with Km.t the place, not the people. Sauneron is still going off the early Egyptologists' notion that the Km.t in *Km.tjw* refers to the country at large. But the point here is that the grammar will not allow *Km.tjw* to mean "the blacks" or "Egyptians" in an ordinary plural sense. Thus, if one was to render Km.t as *Km.tjw*, then the text could not be talking about Km.t "Egypt," but Km.t/Km-Wr "Athribis" the nome because this term only referred to this place, never the country at large. The plural strokes in this rendering of Km.t is not part of the spoken form of the word. It can only be rendered Km.t (*km* root + *-t* suffix). The plural strokes and the people are classifiers and are not grammatical morphemes. The plural strokes are only associated with the *-t* suffix of the word. The seated man and woman are used here to convey the concept of a nation; a political entity. The word doesn't describe any aspect of the inhabitants of Km.t.[48]

I can only recall one other dictionary entry where the authors mistake the Z2 plural strokes classifier ı ı ı as a grammatical morpheme in a place-name and that is with the entry *j3.t-sẖ.tjw* e. "Ort od. Arbeitersiedlung" (place of worker's settlement) (Hanning, 1995: 1297) [Hayes, Pap. Late MK, 72, 83, pl. VI]. Besides there being no evidence of this being a nisbe form of *sẖ.t* via the graphemes, the primary text doesn't support such a rendering either. The following is from the *Thesaurus Linguae Aegyptiae*:[49]

> *3] wḏ, w- [nswt] n (j) m (,j) -r'-n ', t ṯ3, tj [(j) m (,j) -r'] - ḥw, t-wr, t-6 ꜥnḫ, w m =k jni.t[w] [n] [=k] [wḏ,w] [pn] [n(,j)] [bnswtb] [4] r rḏi.t rḫ =k n,t.t [ᵇsprᵇ].n ẖtm(,tj)-bj(,tj) (j)m(,j)-r'-3ḥ,wt-n-n',t-rs(,j)t [jb-j]ꜥ(,w) [5] r-ḏd [ᵇmṯ3.(Pl.)ᵇ] [ᵇmᵇ] [ᵇprᵇ] =¿[j]? m ḏ3i.t r(m)ṯ n(.w) ẖnw m ṯ3[,wt] r j3,t-[sẖ],tw*
>
> Königlicher Befehl an den Vorsteher der Pyramidenstadt, Wesir und Vorsteher der sechs Häuser Anchu: Siehe, es ist dieser Befehl des Königs zu dir gebracht worden, um dich wissen zu lassen, dass der Siegler des Königs von OÄ u.UÄ und Vorsteher der Äcker der südlichen Stadt .... (der Sohn des?) Ibi-jau bittend mit den Worten gekommen ist: 'Unverschämte (?) in meinem Haus (?) transportieren Leute meines Haushaltes, indem sie (sie) wegbringen nach Iat-sechtu.'
>
> [Royal command to the chief of the pyramid city, vizier and head of the six houses of Anchu: See, it has been brought to you this command of the king, to let you know that the sealer of the king of OÄ u.UÄ and head of the fields of the southern city .... (the son of?) Ibi-jau has come pleading with the words: 'Outrageous (?) In my house (?) transport people of my household by taking them to Iat-sechtu.']

The name *j3.t-sẖ.t* is being used here simply as a location, which is a settlement for workers (Cf. *sẖ.tj* "fieldworker, peasant, fowler" [Wb 4, 231.15-232.7; FCD 240]). The decree is requesting that people from the royal house be taken < *r* > "to" *j3.t-sẖ.t*. Given that the location is a settlement place for workers, it explains the seated man and woman glyphs because they are often used together in words for "serfs" (e.g. *mr.wt* "serfs; underlings" [Wb 2, 106.11-20; FCD 111]). Thus, I argue that the people

48 Compare this form with another found in the Book of the Dead that has the seated *nṯr* divine classifier: *km.t* (Budge, 1911: 410a). Are we to then interpret this form as "the black land gods" or "the black people gods?"

49 http://aaew.bbaw.de/tla/servlet/GetTextDetails?u=imhotep06&f=0&l=0&db=0&tc=18734

classifiers are conveying that this is a location of field-workers, farmers, craftsmen, etc. However, there is no grammatical feature of the word to indicate that it is dealing with people that would have been spoken verbally. Instead, the classifiers are included to bring about an expanded context only for the written form. Given that *sẖ.t* and *km.t* are cognates, we can apply the same logic to Km.t . This rendering would point to Km.t as an agrarian society/nation given the fact that *km.t* means "field, irrigated land, wet lands, etc." (see Imhotep 2014, 2016, 2019).

There is one other entry where a place-name is terminated by the seated man and woman sign: *tꜣ-mrj*  "Ägypten = die Bewohner Ägyptens. Seit D.19 auch wie nebenstehend" ("Egypt = the inhabitants of Egypt. Since Dynasty 19…") [Budge 815b[50]; Wb 5, 224.5-6]. We can see via the WB entry that Erman & Grapow are forced to recognize that the word *tꜣ-mrj* is written in a way that it has to be read as "Egypt" in the singular. However, given the people classifiers, and the context of the original text, it has to be interpreted as the "inhabitants of Egypt." This appears to be the only case of this I could find. But notice that, unlike the word *Km.t*  [Wb 5, 127.20], this rendering of *tꜣ-mrj* is not transliterated by either Budge or Erman & Grapow with the nisbe plural marker, i.e. *tꜣ-mr(j).tjw*. One has to wonder about the inconsistency here.

That the plural stroke classifier doesn't always render the word plural is further confirmed in an XVIII Dynasty rendering of *Km.t*  "Athribis" (Vernus, 1978: 348). Here the word Km.t is not a rendering of the country, but of the nome *Km-Wr*. See also a NK rendering of *Km.t-wr(t)*  (Vernus, 1978: 349). We see the collective strokes terminating the place-name, which can only be rendered as the place > abstract/ collective classifier. The same applies to Km.t . The nome *Km-Wr* was home of the worship of the sacred bull of Osiris. It is the presence of the bull glyph that distinguishes *km.t-wr.t* from Km.t the nation. That the Z2  plural strokes is to be seen as a collective classifier is echoed by Vernus (1978) as can be seen in the following passage.

> Des lors la confusion avec le collectif *kmt* "les bovins noirs" (cf. infra), devient possible, d'ou, deja sous le regne d'Amenophis III, la graphie  (Doc. 188). Fecht a vu dans la graphie  (doc. 255) l'indice que le nom d'Athribis se prononcait a peu pres comme le pluriel de km "noir", represente en Copte par les formes ⲕⲁⲙⲁⲩⲉⲓ, ⲭⲁⲙⲉⲩ. Mais en comparant cette graphie avec les graphies analogues, et dont Fecht ne fait pas etat, telles  (296), (310),  (55) et peut-etre  (235), malgre sa date tardive, on peut penser que ce sont des graphies etymologiques, greffees sur une forme, elle-meme confondue avec le collectif kmt, les signes  marquant le collectif et non le pluriel. Ceci dit, certains pluriels coptes proviennent d'un collectif en ancien egyptien. Mais les quelques graphies influencees par le demotique (section G) ne favorisent guere l'hypothese de Fecht.
>
> [From then on the confusion [i.e. of Km.t the nation] with the collective *kmt* "the black cattle" (Cf. infra), becomes possible, whence, under the reign of Amenophis III, the grapheme 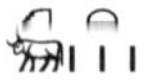 (Doc.188). Fecht saw in the graph  (255) the clue that the name of Athribis was pronounced almost like the plural of *km* "black", represented in Coptic by the forms ⲕⲁⲙⲁⲩⲉⲓ, ⲭⲁⲙⲉⲩ. But by comparing this graph with the similar written forms, and of which Fecht does not show, such as  (296), (310),  (55) and perhaps  (235), despite its late date, one can think that they are etymological graphs, grafted onto a form, itself confused with the *kmt* collective, the  sign marking the collective and not the plural. That said, some Coptic plurals come from an old Egyptian collective. But the few graphemes influenced by the demotic (section G) do not favor the hypothesis of Fecht.] (Vernus, 1978: 352-353)

Thus, we can no longer make the argument that Km.t , as depicted in the Kahun papyrus, is a nisbe plural because the word is not a plural but a singular collective in the same way that the term *America* is a singular collective.

50 Budge simply defines this term as "the people of the land of the Nile-flood, i.e., the Egyptians."

Conclusion

The governing interest of this chapter was to present a working hypothesis for the origin and evolution of the I6 *km* hieroglyph used in the place-name Km.t . We proposed, in agreement with Alassandra Nibbi (1981, 1983), that the I6 glyph evolved from an archaic representation of a mound with vegetation sprouting from it, to a stylized depiction of one side of the bank of the Nile River with vegetation sprouting along the bottom edges starting in the MK. The MK variant of *km* was adapted from the Aa15 *gs* hieroglyph used to write words meaning "half" or "side." We note that the argument for the origin and evolution of the I6 *km* grapheme is a totally separate argument from the linguistic etymology of the place-name *km.t*. There is no *a priori* correlation between the two concepts. The purpose of our analysis was to examine first the nature of the *km* grapheme on its own merits as a step in the process of possibly identifying any correlations with the place-name Km.t. The words Km.t "Egypt" and *km* could be homonyms, which is why the I6 glyph was used (via the rebus principle) to write Km.t. Each argument must be established independently of each other, on their own merits, and then brought together for further analysis after the initial independent research is complete. The full analysis of the etymology of the place-name Km.t is forthcoming in Imhotep (2019).

We then examined and reaffirmed the argument in Imhotep (2014) that the O49 hieroglyph is a representation of two irrigation channels bounded graphically within a circle. The importance of this argument goes to the point that the place-name Km.t is primarily classed in a category of irrigated land for farming. This is confirmed by the various representations of the place-name Km.t with the terminating classifiers for irrigated land: i.e., , , and . Given that the N23 , N36 , and O49 classifiers interchange, and are graphical variants of each other, the word Km.t can only be understood within the context of a type of land suitable for farming and life. It is within this context that the form must be understood. The form found in the MK Kahun papyrus is a rare form and may be found in one other text. 99% of all representations of the place-name Km.t "Egypt" is terminated by either N23 , N36 , and O49 (with the O49 being the most dominant). Thus, the form exists within this larger paradigm of irrigated land, and it is from the irrigated land forms that the form emerges, and not vice-versa. All evidence points to Km.t referring to land with the presence of abundant water with no color connotations. The notion that Km.t means "black soil" or "black people" is not supported by the evidence.

Selected Bibliography

ADEGBOLA, E.A. Ade. (1983). *Traditional Religion in West Africa*. Daystar Press International. Ibadan, Nigeria.

ALLEN, James P. (2005). *The Ancient Egyptian Pyramid Texts*. Society of Biblical Literature.

______ (2010). *Middle Egyptian: An Introduction into the Language and Culture of Hieroglyphs*, 2nd Edition. Cambridge University Press. Cambridge.

______ (2013). *The Ancient Egyptian Language: A Historical Study*. Cambridge University Press. Cambridge.

BATOMA, Atoma. (2006). "African Ethnonyms and Toponyms: An Annotated Bibliography." In: *Electronic Journal of Africana Bibliography*, Vol.10.

BERNAL, Martin. (2006). *Black Athena: The Afroasiatic Roots of Classical Civilization Volume III: the Linguistic Evidence*. Rutgers University Press. New Brunswick, New Jersey.

BILOLO, Mubabinge. (2010). *Invisibilite et Immanence du Createur Imn (Amon-Amun-Amen-Iman-Zimin): Example de la Vitalite de l'Ancien Egyptien ou CiKam dans le Cyena Ntu*. Publications Universitaires Africaines. Munich-Kinshasa-Paris.

______ (2008). *Meta-Ontologie Egyptienne du –IIIe millenaire Madwa Meta-Untu: Tum-Nunu ou Sha-Ntu* (APA. I.8). Munich-Kinshasa-Paris.

______ (2011). *Vers un Dictionnaire Cikam-Copte-Luba: Bantuite du vocabulaire egyptien-copte dans les essays de Homburger et d'Obenga*. Publications Universitaires Africaines. Germany.

BUDGE, E.A. Wallis. (1904). *The Gods of the Egyptians: or Studies in Egyptian Mythology*. 2 vols. Open Court. London and Methuen and Chicago.

______ (1908). *The Book of the Kings of Egypt: Dynasties I-XIX*. Kegan Paul, Trench, Trubner & Co., Ltd., London.

______(1898). *Book of the Dead: A Vocabulary of Hieroglyphs*. Paternoster House. London.

______(1911). *A Vocabulary of Hieroglyphs to the Theban Recension of the Book of the Dead, 2nd Edition*. Kegan Paul, Trench, Trubner & CO., Ltd.

______ (2003). *Egyptian Hieroglyphic Dictionary, Vol.1 and II*. Kessinger Publishing, LLC. New York, NY.

BUNSON, Margaret. (2002). *Encyclopedia of Ancient Egypt. Revised Edition*. Facts on File, Inc. New York, NY.

CHAZAN, R., HALLO, W.W., and SCHIFFMAN, L.H. (1999). *Ki Baruch Hu: Ancient Near Eastern, Biblical, and Judaic Studies in Honor of Baruch A. Levine*. Eisenbrauns. Winona Lake, IN.

DIOP, Chiekh A. (1991). *Civilization or Barbarism: An authentic anthropology*. Lawrence Hill Books. Brooklyn, NY.

______ (1974). *African Origin of Civilization: Myth or Reality*. Lawrence Hill & Co.

______ (1977). *Parenté génétique de l'égyptien pharaonique et des langue snégro-africaines: processus de sémitisation*. Les Nouvelles Éditions Africaines. Ifan-Dakar.

______ (1987). *Precolonial Black Africa: A Comparative Study of the Political and Social Systems of Europe and Black Africa, from Antiquity to the Formation of Modern States*. Lawrence Hill Company. Westport, CT.

______ (1989). *The Cultural Unity of Black Africa: The Domains of Patriarchy and Matriarchy in Classical Antiquity*. Karnak House. UK.

ERMAN, Adolph & Grapow, Hermann. (1971). *Wörterbuch der Aegyptischen Sprache im Auftrage der deutschen Akademien hrsg Bd. I-V*. Unveränderter Nachdruck. Berlin.

FAULKNER, R.O. (1962). *A Concise Dictionary of Middle Egyptian*. Griffith Institute, Ashmolean Museum. Oxford.

FISCHER, Henry G. (1999). *Ancient Egyptian Calligraphy: A Beginner's Guide to Writing Hieroglyphs*, 4th Edition. The Metropolitan Museum of Art. New York, NY.

GOELET, Ogden. (1999). "Kemet and Other Egyptian Terms for Their Land." In: R. Chazan, W.W. Hallo, L.H. Schiffman (Eds). *Ki Baruch Hu: Ancient Near Eastern, Biblical, and Judaic Studies in Honor of Baruch A. Levine*. Eisenbrauns. Winona Lake, Indiana. pp. 23-42.

IMHOTEP, Asar. (2014). "A Lesson in Egyptian Determinatives: The Case of KMT." Self-Published.

______ (2016). *Nsw.t Bjt.j (King) in Ancient Egyptian: A lesson in paronymy and leadership*. Madu-Ndela Press. Philadelphia, PA.

______ (2019). *Aaluja, Vol. II: Cyena-Ntu Religion and Philosophy*. Madu-Ndela Press. Philadelphia, PA.

LIENHARDT, Godfrey. (1961). *Divinity and Experience: The Religion of the Dinka*. Oxford University Press. London.

MBOLI, Jean-Claude. (2010). *Origine des langues africaines: Essai d'application de la méthode comparative aux langues africaines anciennes et modernes*. L'Harmattan. Paris.

NIBBI, Alessandra. (1997). *Some Geographical Notes on Ancient Egypt: A Selection of Published Papers, 1975-1997. Discussions in Egyptology*. Oxford.

______ (1981). *Ancient Egypt and Some Eastern Neighbors*. Noyes Press. Mill Road, NJ.

OBENGA, Theophile. (2004). *African Philosophy: The Pharaonic Period 2780-330 BC*. Per Ankh Publishing. Senegal.

______ (1992). *Ancient Egypt & Black Africa: A Student's Handbook for the Study of Ancient Egypt in Philosophy, Linguistics & Gender Relations*. Karnak House. London

______ (2007). *Ancient Egyptian and Modern Yorùbá: Phonetic Regularity*. In Ankh Journal #16. Per Ankh. Paris, France.

ODUYOYE, Modupe. (1996). *Words and Meaning In Yorùbá Religion: Linguistic Connections Between Yorùbá, Ancient Egyptian and Semitic*. Karnak Publishing. London.

______ (1984). *The Sons of the Gods and the Daughters of Men: An Afro-Asiatic Interpretation of Genesis 1-11*. Oribis Books. Maryknoll, MY.

PETRIE, W. M. Flinders, J. H. Walker, and E. B Knobel. (1908). *Athribis*. School of archaeology in Egypt. London.

SAMBU, Kipkoeech A. (2008). *The Kalenjiin People's Egypt Origin Legend Revisited: Was Isis Asiis?* 2nd Edition. Longhorn Publishers. Nairobi, Kenya.

______ (2011). *The Misiri Legend Explored: A Linguistic Inquiry into the Kalenjiin People's Oral Tradition of Ancient Egypt*. University of Nairobi Press. Nairobi, Kenya.

SCHENKEL, Wolfgang. "Color terms in ancient Egyptian and Coptic," In: Rober E MacLaury, Gailina V. Paramei, Don Dedrick (Hg.), *Anthropology of Color. Interdisciplinary multilevel modeling*, 2007, pp. 211-228.

VAN DER MOLEN, Rami (2000). *A Hieroglyphic Dictionary of Egyptian Coffin Texts*, (Leiden, Boston, Koln: Brill), 2000.

VAN SERTIMA, Ivan. (Ed.). (1986). *Great African Thinkers: Cheikh Anta Diop*. The Journal of African Civilizations, Ltd., Inc. New Brunswich, NJ.

VERNUS, Pascal. (1978). *Athribis, textes et documents relatifs* à la *géographie, aux cultes, et à l'histoire d'une ville du delta égyptien* à *l'époque pharaonique. Institut français d'archéologie orientale du Caire*. France.

WICKER, F.D.P. (1990). *Egypt and the Mountains of the Moon*. Antony Rowe Ltd. Chippenham, Wilts.

WILKINSON, Richard H. (2003). *The Complete Gods and Goddesses of Ancient Egypt*. Thames & Hudson. New York, NY.

WILKINSON, Toby. A. H. (2001). *Early Dynastic Egypt*. Routledge, Inc. New York, NY.

______ (2003). *Genesis of the Pharaohs: Dramatic new discoveries that rewrite the origins of ancient Egypt*. Thames and Hudson, Ltd. London.

WOODCOCK, Taylor B. (2014). *Noticing Neighbors: Reconsidering Ancient Egyptian Perceptions of Ethnicity*. (Unpublished Master's Thesis), The American University in Cairo. Cairo.

Websites

Beinlich Egyptian Online Dictionary
http://www.fitzmuseum.cam.ac.uk/er/beinlich/beinlich.html (German)

Canaanite Dictionary
http://canaanite.org/

Dictionnaire ciLuba
http://www.ciyem.ugent.be/ (French)

Kalenjiin Online Dictionary
http://africanlanguages.com/kalenjin/

Meeussen's Proto-Bantu Reconstructions
http://linguistics.berkeley.edu/CBOLD/Docs/Meeussen.html

Online Etymological Dictionary
http://www.etymonline.com

Online Twi Dictionary:
http://www.twi.bb/

Proto-SBB (P. Boyeldieu, P. Nougayrol& P. Palayer 2004); La liste de Swadesh pour le proto-SBB (Sara-Bongo-Bagirmi, branche Soudan Central des langues Nilo-Sahariennes)
http://sumale.vjf.cnrs.fr/NC/Public/pdf/swadesh_SBB.pdf

Thesaurus Linguae Aegyptiae
http://aaew.bbaw.de/

Tower of Babel
http://starling.rinet.ru/

Yorùbá Dictionary
http://www.Yorùbádictionary.com/

Chapter 4: The Rōmetch of Kemet: Preliminary Notes

Sonjedi Ankh Ra

1.1. Context:

This article was written in preparation for the 36th Annual Ancient Kemetic (Egyptian) Studies Conference (2019) organized by the Association for the Study of Classical African Civilizations (A.S.C.A.C). The focus of this essay is to address what the Kemetic people called themselves, which is *rmṯ ny Km.t* "the people of Kemet," within the context of the larger discourse concerning the meaning of the place-name *Km.t*. In order to get the meaning of the self-identifier *rmṯ ny Km.t* with greater semantic insight, it will be necessary to assess each term independently. This will provide the reader with a broader sense of the overall cultural meaning using a comparative linguistic analysis. The term *rmṯ n(y) Km.t* (Wb., II, 423) consists of three parts: *rmṯ* "man, person, human, mankind, people" (Faulkner, 1999, p. 149; Obenga, 1993, p. 319-20), *n(y)* "of", and *Km.t* (Kmt, the country). It survives in Coptic as ⲣⲙⲛⲕⲏⲙⲉ (Černy, 1976, pp. 136). The following is an excerpt from a larger forthcoming treatment of the subject.

2.1. The term *rmṯ*

In its singular form, *rmṯ* "man" (Wb., II, 421.9; Obenga, 1993, p. 316; Ra, 1995, p. 80)) is written in a number of ways: e.g., *rmṯ,* the full phonetic form without the determinative (semantic) signs; *rm(ṯ),* a shortened form with the *t* or *ṯ* signs omitted with no determinative sign; *rm(ṯ),* another short form omitting the *t* or *ṯ* signs with no determinative. There are shortened forms in which the *m* phonogram and determinatives are omitted: e.g., *r(m)ṯ,* *r(m)t,* and *r(m)ṯ.* Rometch (*rmṯ*) in its plural form is written as . In Coptic *rmṯ* is rendered ρωμε (rōme) in general.

2.2. Attestations of *rmṯ* in selected texts

The chart below lists various spellings and applications of the word from selected texts spanning from the First Golden Age to the Late Period of Dynastic *Km.t*. The left column lists the form of the word as shown in the selected passage. The reader will encounter it in the horizontal right-to-left direction; , the vertical right-to-left direction , and the broader horizontal right-to-left .

Form of the word *rmṯ*	Usage in the text	Textual Source
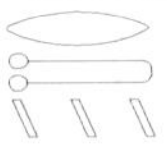	*hꜣ ḥtpwt nṯr i. ḥḏ ḥr rmṯ ḥꜥi ib nṯrw.* the *Ntr*'s contentment will descend, the face of people will brighten, and the *Ntrs*' heart will become aroused.	PT Pepi 523 (PT 581, line 11)
	*sḏm r.k [ḥꜣt(i)-ꜥ]* *mi.k nfr ḏdm n rmṯ* So, listen, high official: Look, it is good for people to listen.	Shipwrecked Sailor, Episode 16, columns 181-182
	*smꜣ.n.i rmṯ im.s m ḫpš.i* *m pḏt.i m nmtwt.i m sḫrw.i iḳrw* I killed some of its people by my strong arm, By my bow, by my strides, by my accomplished plans.	The Story of Sinuhe, Episode 13, Columns 104-106
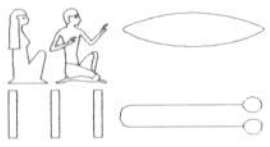	*rdi.in ṯt(i) nis.t(w) nꜣy.f n ẖrdw* *m ḫt ꜥrḳ.f sḫr rmṯ,* *bit.sn m iit ḥr.f* So, the *Djati* had his boys summoned after he came to understand the manner of people, their nature being what had come upon him.	The Instructions of Kagemni's Father, Conclusion, Column 2, lines 3-4.
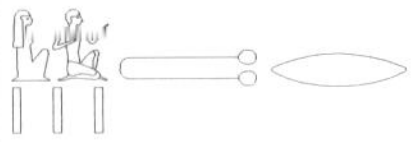	*irrt iꜣw n rmṯ, bin.(w) m ḫt nbt* *fnd ḏbꜣ.(w) ni ssn.n.f* *n tnw ꜥḥꜥ ḥmst* What old age does to people is bad in every respect; The nose is stopped up and cannot breathe for the effort of standing and sitting.	The Instructions of Ptahhotep, Introduction, lines 20-23
	*im.k jir ḫr m rmṯ* You should not make plans by people	Instructions of Ptahhotep, Maxim 5, line 99

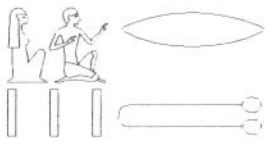	*ỉr wwn.k ḥnꜥ rmṯ,* *ỉr n.k mr n kfꜣ-ib* If you are with people, make a defendant a confident for yourself.	Instruction of Ptahhotep, Maxim 13, lines 232-233
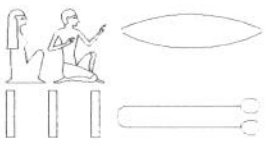	*sbꜣ wr r ꜣḫt n.f,* *sḫpr šzp.f m ḥr(i) ib rmṯ* Teach a great man what is useful for him, Create his acceptance in people's midst.	Instruction of Ptahhotep, Maxim 26, line 399
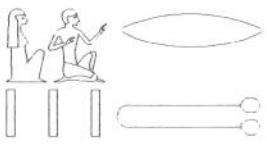	*rwi sḫꜣ.snw m r n rmṯ* *mꜥ nfr n ṯꜣzw.snw* Their memory will dance in the mouth of people Because of the perfection of their phrases	Instructions of Ptahhotep, Conclusion, line 510-511
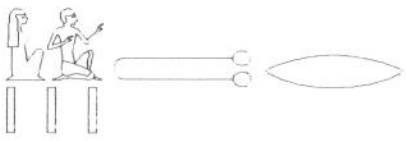	*iḫ ḏd rmṯ mꜣꜣt(i).snw mitt is pfꜣ pw* then people who will see the like say; "Look that is it"	Instruction of Ptahhotep, Conclusion, lines 600-601
	*iw.in [r.f sḫti pn]* *ḥr wꜣt nt rmṯ nbt* So, the peasant came on the path of all people	The Discourses of Khnumanpu, the Eloquent Peasant, Episode 3, lines 31-32
	*ḏd.in nmti-nḫt.(w) pn* *in pꜣ pw ḫn n mdt ḏdw rmṯ* *dm.tw rn n ḫwrw ḥr nb.f* So, Nemtinakht said, "In fact, this is the phrase people say: 'A poor man's name is uttered only because of his *nb*	The Discources of Khnumanpu, the Eloquent Peasant, Episode 3, lines 49-51
	*rḫ ḫt n rmṯ nbt* *in ḫm.k m hꜣw.i* Most knowledgeable of all people, Are you aware of my circumstances?	The Discourses of Khnumanpu, the Eloquent Peasant, Episode 7, lines 165-166

	*sḏm r.k n.i* *mi.k nfr sḏm n rmṯ* *šms hrw nfr smẖ mḥ* So, listen to me; Look, it is good for people to listen: Follow a good time, forget care.	The Debate Between a Man and his *Ba*, the *Ba*'s 3rd Speech, lines 67-68
	*iw mꜣ.n.i zt himt im.f* *nn s(i) m ḥmw rmṯ* I saw a woman in it, who was not a human being.	The Herdman's Tale, lines 3-4
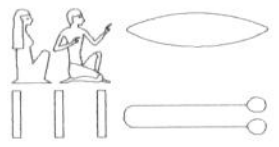	*wrwi nb n niwt.f* *wꜥ ḥḥ pw* *nḏsw pw kwi ẖꜣw rmṯ* How great is the *nb* for his town! He is one in a million; other thousands of people are lesser people.	Hymns to Khakaure Senwoseret III, Hymn 3, Column 2, line 11
	*šẖpr.n.i nṯrw m fdt.i* *rmṯ m rmyt n irit.i* I created the *Nṯrw* from my sweat, and humans from the tears of my eye.	Coffin Texts, Utterance 1130
	*n iri.i isft r rmṯ* I have not done disorder to people.	Book of Going Forth into the Day, Papyrus of Nu, (Pap. British 10, 477), Sheet 22
	*-nw r pꜣ mrwt ⌊n pf(ꜣ) nb m…⌋* *tw.f di bꜣk n.f nꜣy.f rmṯ* -ly on account of the love of [that master (?)…] and he will cause his men to work for him in accordance with the their […	P. Brooklyn 47.218.135, Column 2, line 16

2.3. Presence of *rmṯ* in Negro-Egyptian (Cyena-Ntu) languages (Bilolo, pp. 201., Mboli, pp, 213., Obenga, pp. 316-7).

LANGUAGE	TRANSLITERATION/ VOCALIZATION	MEANING	SOUND CORRESPONDENCES
R3-ny-Kmt (Cikam): Old Egyptian	*rmṯ*	Sing. "man, woman, person" Pl. "people, men, women"	r-m
R3-ny-Kmt (Cikam): Middle Egyptian	*rmṯ*	Sing. "man, woman, person" Pl. "people, men, women"	r-m
R3-ny-Kmt (Cikam) Late Egyptian	*rmṯ*	Sing. "man, woman, person" Pl. "people, men, women"	r-m
Coptic: Sahidic dialect	ρωμε (*rōme*)	"man, people"	r-m
Coptic Akhmimic dialect	ρωμε (*rōme*)	"man, people"	r-m
Coptic: Bohairic dialect	ρωμι (*rōmı*)	"man, people"	r-m
Coptic: Fayumic dialect	(*lōmi*)	"man, people"	r-m :l-m
Sango	*lò*	"he, she"	r-m : l-ø
Soomaali	*lab*	"male"	r-m : l-b
Nuer	*răm*	"man, individual, someone"	r-m: r-m
Azer	*reme*	"child" (semantic transfer)	r-m : r-m
Rendille	*'áram*	"husband"	r-m : r-m
Cokobo	*ù-romò*	"person"	r-m : r-m
Moro	*ò-rom*	"person"	r-m : r-m
Sanga (Bantu)	*ò-romò*	"person"	r-m : r-m
Janji	*(vanò-) roma*	"man"	r-m : r-m
Nkoya (Lunda)	*-rúmè*	"man"	r-m : r-m
Mbochi	*o-lómi*	"husband, man, male"	r-m : l-m
Kikongo	*n-lúmi*	"husband, man, male"	r-m : l-m
Teke	*lúmi, o-lúm*	"husband, man, male"	r-m : l-m
Ndumu	*o-lumu*	"husband, man, male"	r-m : l-m
Mbede	*o-lumi*	"husband, man, male"	r-m : l-m
Duma	*mu-lumi*	"husband, man, male"	r-m : l-m
Ciluba	*mu-lùmɛ*	"husband, man, male"	r-m : l-m
Kisongye	*mu-lume*	"husband, man, male"	r-m : l-m
Mbala	*lúmi*	"husband, man, male"	r-m : l-m
Topoke (Eso)	*lóme*	"husband, man, male"	r-m : l-m
Pende	*mu-lumi*	"husband, man, male"	r-m : l-m
Mbunda	*-lúmè*	"husband, man, male"	r-m: l-m
Buma	*mu-lúm*	"husband, man, male"	r-m : l-m

Gojjam	*á-lema*	"husband, man, male"	r-m : l-m
Amo	*-limè*	"husband, man, male"	r-m : l-m
Mpongwe	*o-nómè*	"husband, man, male"	r-m : n-m
Lele (Kasai)	*numa*	"husband, man, male"	r-m : n-m
Fang	*on-nôm*	"husband, man, male"	r-m : n-m
Tetala	*ómi*	"husband, man, male"	r-m : ø-m
Lomongo	*b-óme*	"husband, man, male"	r-m : ø-m
Ntomba	*bo-óme*	"husband, man, male"	r-m : ø-m
Tsogho	*m-ome*	"husband, man, male"	r-m : ø-m
Mbe	*m-óm*	"husband, man, male"	r-m : ø-m

References:

Allen, J. P. (2010). *Middle Egyptian: An Introduction to the Language and Culture of Hieroglyphs.* (2nd ed. Revised). Cambridge: Cambridge University Press.

________. (2015). Middle Egyptian Literature: Eight Literary Works of the Middle Kingdom. Cambridge: Cambridge University Press.

Bilolo, M. (2011). *Vers un Dictionnaire Cikam-Copte-Luba: Bantuïé du Vocabularire Égyptien-Copte dans les Essais de Homburger et d'Obenga.* Germany: African University Studies.

Breasted, J. H. (1916). *Ancient Times: A History of the Early World: An Introduction to the Study of Ancient History and the Career of Early Man.* Boston, MA: Ginn and Company.

Budge, E.A. (1910). *The Chapters of Coming Forth by Day or the Theban Recension of the Book of the Dead* (2nd ed.). London: Kegan Paul, Trench, Trübner & Co.

Černy, J. (1976). *Coptic Etymological Dictionary.* Cambridge: Cambridge University Press.

Clarke, J. H. (1986). Africa and the Ancient World. In Maulana Karenga & Jacob Carruthers (Eds.), *Kemet and the African Worldview: Research, Rescue and Restoration.* Los Angeles, CA: University of Sankore Press.

Diop, C. (1974). *The African Origin of Civilization: Myth or Reality.* Chicago, IL: Lawrence Hill Books.

El-Daly, O. (2005). *Egyptology: The Missing Millennium: Ancient Egypt in Medieval Arabic Writings.* California: Left Coast Press.

Faulkner, R. (1998). *The Egyptian Book of the Dead: The Book of Going Forth by Day* (2nd ed.). San Francisco: Chronicle Books.

Gardiner, A. (2007). *Egyptian Grammar: Being an Introduction to the Study of Hieroglyphs.* Oxford: Griffith Institute.

Iry-Maat, W. (2015). *A Beginner's Introduction to Medew Netcher: The Ancient Egyptian Hieroglyphic System.* United States of America: Heka Multimedia.

Karenga, M. (2006). *Maat: The Moral Ideal in Ancient Egypt: A Study in Classical African Ethics.* Los Angeles: University of Sankore Press.

Mboli, J. C. (2010). *Origine des langues africaines: Essai d'application de la méthode comparative aux langues africaines anciennes et modernes.* Paris: L'Harmattan.

Obenga, T. (1993). *Origine Commune de L'Égyptien Ancien du Copte et des Langues Negro-Africaines Modernes: Introduction* à *la Linguistique Historique Africaine.* Paris: L'Harmattan.

Ra, A. (1995). *Let the Ancestors Speak: Removing the Veil of Mysticism from Medu Netcher.* Temple Hills, MD: JOLM International, Inc.

Fig. 1: Scene from Rameses III tomb 'table of nations'. Depicted are the *rmṯ* "Egyptians" as evidenced by the name written in between the figures.

12882451R00052

Made in the USA
Monee, IL
30 September 2019